WHAT IS PRAGMATISM?

WHAT IS PRAGMATISM?

BY

JAMES BISSETT PRATT, Ph.D.

ASSISTANT PROFESSOR OF PHILOSOPHY
IN WILLIAMS COLLEGE

New York
THE MACMILLAN COMPANY
1909

All rights reserved

Norwood Press
J. S. Cushing Co. — Berwick & Smith Co.
Norwood, Mass., U.S.A.

PREFACE

DURING the spring of 1908 I received an invitation from Mr. Stephen F. Weston to give a course of six lectures the following summer at the Glenmore Summer School, and to choose my own subject. Unfortunately for the school, as it turned out, I decided to make use of the opportunity to say certain things about pragmatism that had long been stirring in my soul; and "Pragmatism, A Critique," was, accordingly, advertised in the circular of the school as the subject of my lectures. I say my choice was unfortunate for the school, for when, after a twenty-mile drive into the heart of the Adirondacks, I reached Glenmore, I found that the patrons of the school had to a man (and almost to a woman) postponed their arrival to the following week, and it looked as if Mr. Weston and myself would constitute the bulk of the audience.   By the help of the neighbors, however, we managed to corral several philosophers who were known to be at large in the mountains, and several lovers of philosophy, who by their kindly interest and helpful suggestions more than made up for the paucity of their numbers.   The purpose of the publication of this book is, therefore, to show those who did *not* go to Glenmore last summer (and this includes a fairly large portion of the human race) how much they missed.

The criticisms of my friends at Glenmore proved decidedly valuable, and the following pages have, therefore, been somewhat recast since I gave the lectures; yet it has seemed advisable to retain the lecture form as best adapted to somewhat popular and informal exposition.   For though I have nowhere allowed the desire for simplicity and popularity to interfere with thoroughness of treatment, and though I have used technical language where exactness demanded it, my aim has been throughout to give an exposi-

tion and critique of pragmatism which the
general reader could follow without too
much effort. I cannot flatter myself that
he will always find the following pages interesting or easy, but if he really cares to know
about pragmatism and hence comes armed
with patience, he will, I hope, find them
clear.

Although the controversy over pragmatism has now been waging for several years,
and although the non-pragmatists have been
quite as numerous and as active as their
opponents, their contributions to the discussion have been confined almost entirely
to the technical periodicals, whereas the
pragmatist side has been presented to the
public in three or four books which have
commanded a fairly wide reading. Of course
the "public" never reads the technical
periodicals, and there is, therefore, a place
for a book which (while not presupposing any
prior knowledge of the subject) shall present,
with some attempt at comprehensiveness and
unity, the position of those who find them-

selves unable to accept the pragmatist view. Two such books have appeared in France, but there is as yet (so far as I am aware) no book in English which has this aim.

It is, of course, with this aim that I have written the following pages. It would be disingenuous in me should I not frankly declare war on pragmatism even in my preface. But I hope my readers will do me the justice to believe me when I say that to criticise pragmatism has been only my secondary object, my chief aim being to *understand* it and to help others to do so. When the movement first began I was an enthusiastic pragmatist, and my enthusiasm lasted until I came to understand clearly what it really meant. And though I am no longer one of its supporters, its charm is still so strong upon me that I am eager to see it completely developed and carefully expressed, and the good seed which indubitably is in it threshed out and separated from the immense amount of chaff which bears its name. Threshing only can save whatever of value there is in it; and I hope my pragmatist friends will at least see in my book a sincere attempt to aid them in our common task of "making our ideas clear."

My thanks are due to the editors of the *Journal of Philosophy, Psychology, and Scientific Methods,* for their courtesy in permitting me to make use (in Lectures II and III) of material taken from two articles of mine which appeared in their *Journal* during the years 1907 and 1908. And most of all I wish to acknowledge with sincere gratitude the invaluable and unfailing assistance, advice, and guidance which I have received from Professor John E. Russell of Williams College. It was at first his intention to collaborate with me upon a book of this nature, but lack of time prevented him from carrying out his part of the plan, — to the very considerable loss of the many who would have read this book had he been its principal author. But the loss has not been absolute; for those of my readers who have

followed the controversy over pragmatism
will recognize that very much of what is
best in this book is due to him.

WILLIAMSTOWN, MASS.,
February 1, 1909.

CONTENTS

LECTURE I

MEANING AND METHOD IN PRAGMATISM

WHAT IS PRAGMATISM?

LECTURE I

MEANING AND METHOD IN PRAGMATISM

I REMEMBER once hearing a professor of "Real Property" in one of our leading law schools discuss very learnedly and at considerable length the question whether any one in the United States really owned any land. To put it in the professor's words, the question was (if I remember aright) whether the title to land was ever actually vested in the individual or whether he was merely an occupant, the real owner being the state. On the one hand, the professor pointed out, the individual could do what he liked with his land, could deed it to whom he pleased and dispose of it in any way that suited him. But, on the other hand, there was the power of eminent domain, the right of the state to condemn the land and take it from him, for a suitable consideration, at any time. This being the case, in whom is the ownership *really* vested?

The conclusion to which most of us came, as I remember it, was that this was one of the mysteries of the law which the mind of man could never fathom. Doubtless the land belonged to some one; in fact, it very obviously belonged either to the individual or to the state. But *to which* of these it *really* belonged was a question which could probably never be answered.

Now if there had been among us at the time a pragmatist philosopher, he would probably have addressed us in some such words as these: "My friends," he would have said, "your difficulty is all of your own making. You think you are puzzling over a very deep problem; but there is really no problem here to puzzle over. What you take for depth is in fact only the muddiness of your own thought. For consider: What you want to know is in whom the ownership of the land is vested. That being the case, your first question should be, What do we *mean* by ownership? And the answer to this is simple enough; namely, the right to do this, that, and the other with the object owned. Enumerate all the things that can be done with land; then the right to do just these things *is* ownership. And once you have enumerated these rights, you have exhausted the meaning of the term. If ownership means anything more than this, what is it? You cannot say. Except in the concrete and practical sense I have defined, '*ownership*' means just nothing at all, — it is a mere term without content. Of course, one's ownership may be more or less limited, according as one has the right to do fewer or more things with the object one 'owns.' Hence, to return to your particular question, the individual owns the land in the sense of being able to dig in it, build on it, sell it, or give it away, etc.; and the state owns it in the sense of being able to take it from the individual if it desires. And so your question answers itself. In short, your insoluble mystery is merely gratuitous mystification of your own making. It seems a mystery only because it is meaningless."

I have used this illustration, drawn from a field at some distance from philosophy, to show how the pragmatist may often succeed in solving our problems for us by simply demonstrating to us that they are no problems at all. Don't seek to solve a question, says pragmatism, until you know what you mean by it. Think so far as possible in concrete terms. Never let yourself be hoodwinked and browbeaten by big words and verbal abstractions. Remember that the meaning of philosophical terms may often be in inverse proportion to their length. Words are but pragmatists' counters; they do but reckon with them; but they are the money of non-pragmatists. Concerning every object of discussion ask the question: *What is it known as? What does it mean to me?* For, as G. H. Lewes has said, and as Aristotle said long before him, *a thing is what it does*. All that it can ever mean is just the difference that it can make to some one. There is no genuine difference that does not *make* a difference.

Well, every pragmatist will tell you this is pragmatism; and I trust all my hearers are good pragmatists. It goes without saying that I am one. Who, indeed, could resist a doctrine so delightfully healthy, clear-cut, simple, and helpful? It has the salt air of the sea in it and the ozone of the mountains. With this philosophy within one's grasp, who would choose to be bound down in servile submission to verbal abstractions, and to spend one's days discussing problems that have no meaning? Rather let us think clearly and to the point, and sign an intellectual Declaration of Independence from all unmeaning concepts. It is not surprising that the new philosophy is advancing victoriously over the land, and that all sorts and conditions of men are joining the procession. In the glow of our loyalty we are willing to march against any foe, under our banner, upon whose ample folds we have written, " Away with Logomachy and Meaningless Abstractions! "

But alas! where is the foe? Who is it that is championing logomachy and meaningless abstractions? If belief in clear thought and the other admirable things named above be pragmatism, are we not all pragmatists? — Indeed, we do not all practice what we preach (not even all the leaders of pragmatism do that), but who would not give his enthusiastic assent to the laudable doctrines and admonitions set out above? — And if we are all pragmatists and there be no foe to fight, the rather disconcerting question presents itself why we should make such a fuss about it. Unless pragmatism has something more distinctive and original to offer, is it really anything more than a new and rather superfluous name for some exceedingly old and common ways of thinking?

Of course pragmatism is more than this, — otherwise it would resemble a Fourth of July oration on "Liberty" in a New England village, or a revival among the sanctified. Pragmatism seeks and claims to be strenuous, militant, — a plan of campaign rather than a celebration or an experience meeting. So much of pragmatism as I have described thus far is only its spirit; but it is in addition to this a definite and technical doctrine or group of doctrines on certain fundamental philosophical questions. "Pragmatism (according to Mr. James) is a temper of mind, an attitude; it is also a theory of the nature of ideas and truth; and finally it is a theory about reality."[1] More specifically, it may be said that pragmatism offers us a theory of *meaning*, a theory of *truth*, and a theory of *knowledge;* that it is trying to work out a theory of *reality;* and that it is also a general point of view or way of looking

[1] Professor Dewey in "What does Pragmatism mean by Practical?" *Jour. of Phil.*, Vol. V, p. 85.

at things, — a way that is in part peculiar to pragmatists, in part adopted by them from a larger tendency or attitude which colors much of contemporary thought. I shall take up each of these things in turn in the following lectures, beginning to-day with a consideration of the pragmatist doctrine of the nature of meaning and of the method of dealing with philosophical problems which pragmatism naturally deduces from that doctrine.

"Meaning" and "method" are, I confess, not intrinsically interesting subjects. I wish I had something more attractive to offer you, but it really is not my fault. I might, of course, give you just a general "point of view" which would, perhaps, not be altogether without interest; but I mean to do no such thing. I mean to treat the technical doctrines of pragmatism in as exact a fashion as I can — any other treatment of them I should consider an insult to my audience. Pragmatism has been defined by its founder as a way "to make our ideas clear";

hence its doctrines must themselves certainly
be clear and capable of exact formulation.
We should not be satisfied — and so far as
we are good pragmatists we cannot be satisfied — with any loose definitions and any
vague *tendencies* and *generalities*. So long
as we allow ourselves to be soothed and
satisfied by them we shall be very far from
making our ideas clear. We must therefore do pragmatism the justice to take it
seriously, to sift the formulations of it given
by the leading pragmatists, and not to rest
satisfied till we see exactly what they mean.
Such a thorough-going examination of pragmatic meaning and method may seem to
some of you at times dry, difficult, and perhaps over-technical. But if you are really
consistent, sincere, and honest pragmatists
at heart, you will not hesitate at any difficulty in the effort to make your ideas clear
and to free yourselves from the power of
mere words and phrases. Those, on the
other hand, who are pragmatists in name
only I am sure will stay behind, content with

" words " and " tendencies," and will continue to throw their caps in air, shouting, " Hurrah for Pragmatism ! " without being over-curious as to what it really is, or why they should make such a noise about it.

Pragmatism may be regarded as the result of two confluent, though not altogether consistent, streams of tendency. The first, and probably the less influential, of these may be traced back as far as Kant's doctrine of the primacy of the practical reason. We cannot, said Kant, *prove* the reality of God, freedom, immortality, and the moral law. But since we are volitional, active, rational beings we have both the right and the duty to *postulate* the reality of these things and whatever else may be essential to moral action. It is indeed possible that we are not free; but we are bound to act *as if* we were free, and since freedom is essential to morality, it is our duty to believe in it.

Practically this same brave moral doctrine was revived and reformulated in 1896 by Professor James's " Will to Believe,"—a book that has stirred America as have few philosophic works of our generation. In the first essay of the volume (which gave its title to the whole) Professor James points out that faith is itself a force and often makes real its own object; and that when we are faced with genuinely possible alternatives we have a right to accept and believe that one whose acceptance will contribute most to our moral life. Here and elsewhere, moreover, James shows that in morality and metaphysics and religion, as well as in science, we are justified in testing the truth of a belief by its usefulness.

The second and probably the more important source of pragmatism is the modern scientific view of the meaning of hypotheses. Hypotheses, "natural laws," scientific generalizations, etc., are, as most scientists now maintain, merely short-hand expressions of human experience. They are handy ways of telling us what has happened or what we may expect. They are not so much descriptions of an outer and independent "nature " as ways of summarizing and explaining our experience. Their whole meaning is exhausted after they have told us (directly or indirectly) how things act upon us and how we react upon things. That I may be sure not to misrepresent the modern logic of science as pragmatism understands it, let me make use of a sentence from Ostwald, quoted with approval by Professor James in his recent book.

" All realities influence our practice, and that influence is their meaning for us. I am accustomed to put questions to my classes in this way: In what respects would the world be different if this alternative or that were true? If I can find nothing that would become different, then the alternative has no sense." [1]

In a somewhat similar spirit Karl Pearson defines a law of science (or of " nature ") as " a *resumé* in mental shorthand, which replaces for us a lengthy description of the sequences among our sense impressions." [2]

[1] Quoted by James in " Pragmatism," p. 48.
[2] " Grammar of Science," p. 87.

The scientist, in short, sees that his hypotheses and laws ultimately get all their meaning from our experience.   And, moreover, he no longer regards them purely as ends in themselves; rather are they now his *instruments* by the use of which human action may profitably be guided.   Hence he is less concerned than were his predecessors with the question whether his hypotheses are *true;* what concerns him most is their *usefulness*. His great question concerning any proposed generalization is, *Does it work?*   And this for two reasons: in the first place, because its working is practically more important to him than its merely theoretical truth; and secondly, because the only test he has for its truth is its successful working.   Unless it works, he has no reason to believe it true. Moreover, as truth and usefulness are both forms of value, the scientist who has no time nor fondness for what he calls "logic chopping" has a tendency to identify the two, without asking himself too curiously whether his hypothesis is true because it is useful or useful because it is true.

It was from this view of the nature of scientific hypotheses that pragmatism, in the more technical sense, took its rise. The name originated with Mr. C. S. Pierce, who in 1878 published his epoch-making article (for so it turned out to be) entitled " How to make our Ideas Clear."[1] In this paper Mr. Pierce laid down the thesis that the whole meaning of any object consists in the habit or reaction it establishes or induces (directly or indirectly) in us. " Consider what effects which might conceivably have practical bearings we consider the object of our conception to have. Then our conception of these effects is the whole of our conception of the object."[2] The word "practical" Mr. Pierce is here using in its strict and etymological sense, as referring to action.[3] Thus we are told that to develop the meaning of a thought " we have simply to determine what habit it induces, for what a thing means is simply what habit it involves."[4] " There is

---

[1] In the *Popular Science Monthly*, Vol. XII, pp. 286–302.
[2] p. 293.   [3] From the Greek πρᾶγμα, *action*.   [4] p. 292.

no distinction of meaning so fine as to consist in anything but a possible difference of
practice."[1]   Quite in line with this view of
the *practical* nature of meaning is Professor
Dewey's use of the word *idea* as synonymous
with "plan of action" or "intention to act in
a certain way."[2]

Now the assertion (if intended to be taken
literally) that *all* distinction of meaning *consists in* a possible difference of practice cannot
be allowed to go unchallenged.   It may be
true that most concepts and beliefs — or, if
you insist, that *all* concepts and beliefs —
result ultimately in action.   From that it
does not follow that all their meaning *consists in* such resulting action.   Doubtless
much of their meaning does consist in that. —
My concept of an object is largely made up
of the way I should act in its presence.   As
Royce has well said, I do not know the
meaning of "*lion*" if I think it an animal I
might pat on the head, saying, "Nice little

[1] p. 293.
[2] Cf., for instance, *Mind*, Vol. XVI, pp. 335–336, and
Jour. of Phil., Vol. V, p. 88, etc.

subj

lion."— But though this is true, there remains always in our concepts and beliefs a group of characteristics which are not to be reduced to any reactions or habits of our own. These may be of as many sorts as there are kinds of experience or psychic states in addition to action. Sensational and emotional facts are of course the most obvious. The distinction between a red house and a green house does not *consist in* a difference of practice. Even granted there is a difference in practice or "attitude" resulting, that would not *constitute* the whole of the distinction. "Practice" surely cannot be taken to mean the whole of experience. (If it were so taken, Mr. Pierce's expressions about it would become the most absurdly obvious truisms.) But if it be not the whole of experience, there is no good reason for insisting that it is the only type of experience which contributes anything toward the meaning of ideas.

This point is so obvious that I surely need not labor it further. And I am made still more confident that I may be relieved of this

ungrateful task by the fact that Professor
James long ago saw this weakness in Mr.
Pierce's formulation of pragmatism, and
therefore " transmogrified " it (as Pierce
puts it) and laid the foundations of his
own pragmatism in more inclusive terms.
In his famous California Address of August 26, 1898, — which we might almost call
the birthday of pragmatism, — he says: —

" I think myself that it [the principle
of pragmatism] should be expressed more
broadly than Mr. Pierce expresses it. . . .   I
should prefer to express Pierce's principle
by saying that the effective meaning of
any philosophic proposition can always be
brought down to some particular consequence in our future practical experience,
whether active or passive; the point lying
rather in the fact that the experience must
be particular than in the fact that it must
be active."[1] This interpretation of the term
practical as meaning concrete and particular
rather than as referring to action, Pro-

---

[1] *Jour. of Phil.*, Vol. I, p. 674.   Italics mine.

fessor James has consistently maintained
ever since.[1]

Taking this modified and enlarged statement of the pragmatic view of meaning,
let us try to see exactly what it amounts to.
As I understand it, pragmatism aims by it
to do two things. First, it seeks to give
us a definite, exact, and technical doctrine
of the nature of meaning — to show us what
meaning consists in and, therefore, when it
is present and when absent. And, secondly, by means of this doctrine, it aims to
formulate for us a method of choosing our
problems, which shall eliminate for us a
number of meaningless questions and help
us to see what is worth discussing and what
is not. With these aims in view, let us now
examine some of the more carefully worded
statements of the pragmatic doctrine.

In Baldwin's " Dictionary of Philosophy,"
Professor James defines pragmatism as

[1] Cf. his definition of pragmatism in Baldwin's Dictionary
and his article, " The Pragmatic Account of Truth," in the
Phil. Rev. for January, 1908, especially p. 14. Also " Pragmatism," Lecture II, *passim.*

"the doctrine that the whole 'meaning' of a conception expresses itself in practical consequences, consequences either in the shape of conduct to be recommended or in that of experiences to be expected, if the conception be true; which consequences would be different if it were untrue, and must be different from the consequences by which the meaning of other conceptions is in turn expressed. If a second conception should not appear to have other consequences, then it must really be only the first conception under a different name."

The fundamental postulate of "immediate empiricism" (a pseudonym for pragmatism) is, according to Professor Dewey, just this: "that things are what they are experienced *as* being; or that to give a just account of anything is to tell what *that* thing is experienced to be." "The real significance of this principle is that of a method of philosophical analysis. If you wish to find out what any philosophic term means, go to experience and see what it is experienced *as*." [1]

In the same spirit Papini writes: "The meaning of theories consists uniquely in the consequences which those who believe them true may expect from them." [2] Dr. Schiller puts it thus: "To say that a truth has consequences and that what has none is meaningless, means that it has a bearing upon some human interest. Its 'consequences' must be consequences *to* some one *for* some purpose. If it is clearly grasped that the 'truth' with which we are concerned is truth *for man* and that the 'consequences' are human too, it is really superfluous to add either that the consequences must be *practical* or that they must be *good*." [3]

Owing to a misunderstanding of some of the pragmatists' statements, they have

[1] "The Postulate of Immediate Empiricism," *Jour. of Phil.*, Vol. II, pp. 397 and 399.

[2] "Introduzione al Pragmatismo," Leonardo, February, 1907, p. 28.

[3] "Studies in Humanism," p. 5.

been accused of including among the
'consequences' that give meaning only
such as are practical in the ordinary
sense of the word, — *bread and butter* consequences one might call them. Put in
this bald and sweeping way, this criticism
is based on a radical misunderstanding of
pragmatism. All the leading pragmatists
insist that among these 'practical consequences' they include such things as
logical consistency, intellectual satisfaction,
harmony of mental content, etc. James
has more than once made the statement
that to him *practical* means simply *particular* or *concrete;*[1] and Schiller has frequently pointed out that what are commonly
called theoretical consequences are practical in his broad use of the word, and
that, in fact, "all consequences are practical sooner or later."[2] If all consequences
are practical sooner or later, it is at first,
indeed, a little hard to see why so much

---

[1] Cf. *Jour. of Phil.*, Vol. I, p. 674; *Phil. Rev.*, Vol. XVII,
pp. 14 and 15.   [2] " Studies in Humanism," p. 6.

emphasis should be laid upon their being
practical, or why so much ado should be
made over the word; it would seem to be
something like a distinction without a difference, rather useless as a guide or tool,
and hence most unpragmatic. Moreover,
there are passages in which the pragmatists
seem to forget their own broad use of the
word *practical*, and to condemn certain
"intellectualistic" questions as unworthy
of discussion because far removed from
our "practical" needs. And it must also
be added that while the pragmatists usually
recognize the value of our theoretical interests, they insist that in the last analysis
this value is entirely dependent on the
"practical" in the narrower sense of the
term, — that our intellectual activities get
all their worth ultimately from the fact
that they guide and influence the reaction
of the individual upon the environment.
Limited Sense:
This is what Dr. Schiller really has in
mind when he says, "all consequences are
practical sooner or later." It would seem,

therefore, that the "bread and butter" criticism is not altogether without foundation. Of this, however, I hope to have more to say at another time. For the present the important thing for us to note is the fact that pragmatism is not justly open to the charge of completely disregarding our theoretic interests, — no matter how it may, later on, interpret them.

And now let us come to closer quarters with the pragmatic doctrine of meaning. There are one or two points in it which have never been clear to me, and which, so far as I am aware, no pragmatist writer has attempted to clear up. As these points are vital to our problem, I must have more light on them before I know whether I am a pragmatist or not. So let us return for a moment to our definitions. I repeat: According to Professor James, "the meaning of any philosophical proposition can always be brought down to some particular consequence in our future practical experience." According to Dr. Schiller, the "consequences" must be "consequences *to* some one, *for* some purpose." Now I ask (and it is an important question), What does James mean by "*our* experience"? To whom does Schiller refer by the words "*some one*"? Obviously there are three possible interpretations. The pragmatist may mean, namely, that only that concept or theory has meaning which makes a ("practical") difference (1) to me, the individual, or (2) to all human beings of all times, or (3) to all actual or possible rational or sentient beings. If the pragmatist theory is to be of any help to us whatever, we must know which of these three positions it takes. In the lack, therefore, of any authoritative statements on this subject from the pragmatists, let us examine each of these possible positions in turn for ourselves.

The first position suggested above may, I suppose, be dismissed at once. It is most unlikely that any pragmatist will hold that only that has any meaning which has consequences in the shape of conduct or experiences *in his own individual life and mind.*

For even if one should hold so preposterous a position, he could scarcely give it out seriously as a philosophic method. The question whether there will be a railway to the north pole five hundred years hence can certainly not be expressed in consequences to me as an individual, "either in the shape of conduct to be recommended or in that of experiences to be expected." And yet the question certainly has meaning, because its consequences may be expressed in the conduct or experience of some one else. For the same reason various questions of ancient history have meaning, even for me. Nor can we logically stop short of the whole human race, in interpreting the meaning of "some one."

But what justification have we for stopping here? How can we logically disregard the real or possible experiences or any real or possible sentient beings? Would there be no *meaning* in saying that an ichthyosaurus, who perished ages before the birth of the first man, suffered pain or perceived the light? Is there now no *meaning* in Mr. Percival Lowell's assertion that there are sentient and rational beings on Mars? There is, so far as I can see, not a single detail of any human experience that would in any way be different, whichever side of these questions you should take. And yet the questions certainly have a meaning, and have a meaning to us, because they have consequences in the conduct and experiences of real or possible sentient beings; namely, the ichthyosaurus and the Martians.

The consequences which give meaning, therefore, cannot be confined to the human race, but must include all those which occur in the experience of any sentient creatures. If from this, however, we are tempted to conclude that there is nothing unique or original in the doctrine of the pragmatist, he may remind us that we have as yet failed to note one of its most important characteristics. The "consequences" which, according to pragmatism, alone give meaning are "consequences in our *future* practical experience."

It is not past nor present consequences, but "conduct *to be recommended*," "experiences *to be expected*," that count in giving significance to a proposition. A good deal is made, first and last, in various pragmatic writings, of this conception that it is only in the future consequences that meaning resides, and it will therefore be worth our while to consider it in some detail. This we can best do by applying it to a concrete example.[1]

The example I shall choose is the one which appears most often in Professor James's writings[2] as an illustration of the pragmatist doctrine of meaning. "Imagine," says Professor James, "the entire contents of the world to be once for all irrevocably given. Imagine it to end this very moment,

[1] This same emphasis upon the future is implicit (as Professor Montague has shown) in the pragmatic attempt to make truth only a kind of goodness.

[2] It occurs both in the California Address and in "Pragmatism" (from which I here quote it, p. 96), and we would seem, therefore, to be justified in taking it as a typical illustration of pragmatic meaning — provided, of course, that we do not raise against it the criticism forestalled by Professor James himself in his "Pragmatic Account of Truth," *Phil. Rev.*, Vol. XVII, p. 5, note.

and to have no future; and then let a theist
and a materialist apply their rival explana-
tions to its history. The theist shows how
a God made it; and the materialist shows,
and we will suppose with equal success, how
it resulted from blind physical forces. Then
let the pragmatist be asked to choose between their theories. How can he apply
his test if the world is already completed?
Concepts are things to come back into experience with, things to make us look for
differences. But by hypothesis there is to
be no more experience, and no possible differences can be looked for. Both theories
have shown all their consequences, and by
the hypothesis we are adopting these are
identical. The pragmatist must consequently say that the two theories, in spite
of their different-sounding names, mean exactly the same thing, and that the dispute
is purely verbal." [1]

The point of this illustration is, of course,

[1] Professor James adds here a parenthetical sentence
which, if taken as in any sense limiting or modifying his illustration, destroys the entire force of his argument. I have
therefore omitted it.

to show that it is only in *future* consequences that genuine meaning can reside. Now, in the first place, it is important to note that, with the pragmatist view, and under the supposed conditions,— the end of the world, — *any* question of past or present fact would necessarily be unmeaning. The theistic-materialistic controversy is not peculiar in this respect. To say at the end of the world, " Professor James wrote the book ' Pragmatism,' " and to say, " Mr. Bradley wrote it," would mean exactly the same thing, since the consequences are once for all what they are, and no future consequences can be looked for. That this must be true of all questions, no matter how full of meaning they now seem to us, follows necessarily from the very nature of the case, once you admit the pragmatic doctrine. For if all meanings can be brought down to consequences " in our *future* practical experience," and if, by hypothesis, we have no future practical experience, it must follow, as the night the day, that there can no longer be any meaning in anything.

And it must also be noted that this conclusion not only will, according to pragmatism, hold true at the end of the world for all
questions, but that, on the same principles,
it must also hold true of many questions
even now.   To take a very commonplace
example: suppose three gentlemen discussing after dinner the age of the wine they
have been drinking.   One of them says that
it is three years old, one that it is thirteen.
Reasons are given by both, but neither can
prove his point to the satisfaction of the
other.   The dispute is referred to the third
gentleman, who happens to be a pragmatist.
How can he apply his test, since the wine,
having become once for all what it was, has
now been drunk, and the bottle is empty?
Both theories have shown all their consequences, and these are identical.   "The
pragmatist must consequently say that the
two theories, in spite of their different-sounding names, mean exactly the same thing,"
that to say the wine is three years old is only
another way of saying it is thirteen years old,

and that the dispute is purely verbal. In like manner, the date of Sargon I, the authorship of the Pentateuch, the question of the Greek tactics at Salamis, all being without future consequences to us, must be for the pragmatist absolutely meaningless. In short, from history, geology, biology, astronomy, — from every field of human thought, — come questions over which scholars are spending years of research, yet which are certainly even now fully as meaningless as the theistic-materialistic controversy will be at the end of time, and which therefore according to the pragmatist doctrine are purely verbal disputes.[1]

The response may be made that the hypotheses and questions just referred to have pragmatic consequences in the sense of fitting in more or less well with our otherwise

[1] By the above I do not, of course, mean that no pragmatist has a right to a past fact; I simply wish to point out that he has no right to one so long as he sticks to his assertion that all meaning is confined to future consequences, and more especially to the interpretation of this assertion exemplified by James's illustration of the end of the world.

D

grounded beliefs, and hence producing greater
or less mental harmony. But the answer to
this is, in the first place, that this can be the
case only on condition that these questions
and hypotheses *already have meaning*. Their
harmonizing with our other beliefs *presupposes* their meaning and does not *produce*
it, — hence their meaning does not *consist
in* these consequences. And in the second
place, if this answer of the pragmatist holds
of the questions I have suggested, it holds
equally well of the materialistic-theistic controversy at the end of the world and of every
question which rationalistic philosophers are
to-day discussing. There is scarcely a question seriously raised to-day by any school of
philosophy so " intellectualistic " that it is
lacking in consequences of intellectual harmony, hence not one which the pragmatist
formula, if thus broadly interpreted, would
rule out.

Pragmatism must choose between the
broad and the narrow interpretation of its
doctrine. If it chooses the latter, it must

maintain explicitly that only that has meaning which (1) has consequences in the experience or conduct of *us human beings*, or (2) has *future* consequences for some one, or (3) has both. Some of the expressions used by the pragmatists seem clearly to show that they prefer the narrow interpretation. But, as I think must now be clear to you all, this position is untenable. For, to repeat, (1) that obviously has meaning which has consequences to any conceivable sentient creature. Though theism and materialism should have identical consequences for me and for all human beings, they certainly have not for *God* (whether he be real or hypothetical). It makes a difference to God whether He exists or not, even if this be the last moment of time. And there is no more reason for ruling out God's experience or that of the ichthyosaurus or the Martian, or of Jupiter or Thor, than that of Adam or of Sargon I. Surely I know what I mean when I speak of the experiences of Betsy Prig or Sairey Gamp or even those of the

doubly mythological Mrs. Harris.   Whatever
makes a difference to any conceivable sentient
creature has at least some meaning.   And
(2) it is impossible to see why only *future*
consequences should count, and past ones
give no meaning.   If the pragmatist is
unable to get any meaning out of past consequences, or out of consequences to sentient beings who are not human, that is his
misfortune.   But as for the rest of us, we
know perfectly well what we mean when we
say Mars is inhabited, or the birds preceded
the mammals, quite aside from any consequences, future or past, to human beings.
And in like manner, were this the last moment of time we should know perfectly well
what we meant by saying, The world is due
to an intelligent, self-conscious Being, or,
The world is due to the concourse of unconscious atoms ; and we should know also that
these two meanings were altogether different.

It would seem, therefore, that pragmatism
is logically forced to adopt only the broadest
possible interpretation of its doctrine, an

interpretation which could be expressed as follows: the meaning of any conception expresses itself in the past, present, or future conduct or experience of actual or possible sentient creatures. And if this is the pragmatist doctrine, it certainly is sound. But the odd thing about it is that it exhibits pragmatism as (so far forth) nothing but a restatement of idealism. If this be pragmatism, we shall soon find the subjectivists and the pan-psychists joining the procession; yes, even the prophets of the Absolute will be donning pragmatist colors and learning war no more. The lion shall eat straw like the ox; and James and Royce, Dewey and Lotze, Schiller and Bradley (!), shall lie down together. Only the radical realists shall be left out of the love feast.

I do not want to be understood as seeking a cheap and easy victory over pragmatism, nor as desiring to ridicule it. What I want is genuinely to understand it. And I seriously contend that pragmatism either must take the untenable position of denying meaning where meaning obviously is, or else must admit that there is nothing unique in its doctrine. It either stands for an absurdity or else, so far as I can see, it has contributed nothing of importance to the problem in question and has merely repeated the general view of idealism, which it might almost as well have quoted (in somewhat different words, to be sure, but in substance and without all this ado) from any one of several passages in "Appearance and Reality." What shall we say, then, to these things? Is Bradley also among the pragmatists?

If any pragmatist or pragmatist proselyte has consented to follow me thus far, he will probably say at this point, At least pragmatism offers a practical and useful method for determining what philosophic questions are really worth discussing, and by application of this method we shall be enabled to eliminate a large body of worthless and abstract problems which are now lumbering up our minds to no useful purpose. This method, he would probably continue, might be summed up in the rule never to discuss anything unless it has some genuine human interest, unless it makes a real difference to some one.

Now if by this rule pragmatism means, once more, simply the maxim to avoid logomachy, we shall certainly say Amen to its time-honored admonition. But if it means something more than this, we must ask, What is really meant? Truly we should discuss only that which is worth discussing; but who is to determine what this is? And the point upon which we are here most in need of enlightenment is this: Does pragmatism include among its "genuine human interests" the intellectual desire for knowledge for its own sake? If it does not, then we must at least point out the fact that "intellectualistic metaphysics" is not the only thing tabooed. A large proportion of the problems of higher mathematics, history, archæology, astronomy, geology, literary criticism, etc., are as certainly vetoed and forbidden. The courses in our universities must be cut down by half. For in every field of scholarly inquiry there are innumerable questions which awaken no more "responsive active feelings" in "us practical Americans" and call for no more "particular conduct of our own" than do the various theological and metaphysical problems against which the pragmatists inveigh. The distance of the nearest fixed star, the problems of the higher mathematics, the age of the Rig Veda, awaken as little "sense of reality" in most of us as do the various "philosophic propositions that will never make an appreciable difference to us in action." One and all, they are open to the same reproach of not "making any difference" to a living soul — except the difference which comes with the satisfaction of knowing. But by what right, after all, shall these things be declared not worth discussing? Surely every genuine question — every question, that is, which has meaning and is not logomachy — is worth solving to him who wishes to solve it. If you, personally, are not interested in mathematics or metaphysics, by all means steer clear of them. But it is surely unworthy of the broad, human, and empirical spirit that characterizes all true pragmatists to attempt to dogmatize as to what all men shall find or ought to find interesting.

In fact, if the question be thus put, the pragmatists might, perhaps, say that the purely theoretic interest should be taken into account and recognized as one of the things that give problems their value. But if this is the case, again I ask, What problem, then, is ruled out beyond mere verbal disputes which all would rule out? How does the pragmatist rule or method assist us in choosing our problems? Can the pragmatist name us one single problem which philosophers are discussing to-day which should not, on his own showing, be recognized as worth while? Take, as a concrete example, the most extreme case thinkable, — or, letting the pragmatists choose for us, consider the one Professor James has selected as his favorite mark, — the " aseity " of God.[1] The choice was excellent for the purpose, for it seems to interest but few, and the name sounds remote and even absurd. Yet there certainly have been many, and still are some, who would genuinely like to know whether there is a divine Being who derives his existence from himself, or whether everything in the universe, "God" included, is bound on the weary wheel of external derivation. And in spite of the disrepute into which Scholasticism has brought the subject, I think, on the whole, nearly every one of us here would be more genuinely interested in knowing about the attributes of God than about the distances between the fixed stars. Of course the discussion of these theological things is not religion. But to condemn all such discussion because it is not this that "keeps religion going" is like condemning astronomy because it does not give us light and heat.

[1] Cf. James's California Address, *Jour. of Phil.*, Vol. I, pp. 680–681, and "Varieties of Religious Experience," pp. 445–446.

And, to conclude, the whole matter may be put in the form of a dilemma: If, on the one hand, the various questions which pragmatism would taboo are of genuine intellectual interest to any one, they are, on pragmatist principles, worth his investigation and discussion. And if, on the other hand, they are not of interest to any one, it would seem hardly pragmatic to spend breath, ink, and time in attempting to prevent their investigation.

If, therefore, the intellectual desire to know be admitted as a pragmatic interest, I cannot see that pragmatism helps us one whit in the selection of our problems, — unless, indeed, we are to take seriously the implication sometimes given by certain pragmatist writers; namely, that only those topics are worth discussing which are to their taste. This, for instance, is the impression one gets on reading Papini. The pragmatist, he tells us, will "not concern himself with a large part of the classical problems of metaphysics (in particular with

the universal and rational explanation of all
things), which are for him unreal problems
and devoid of meaning. . . .   He will have
an antipathy for all forms of monism . . .
and for the ' reality ' of the ordinary man. . . .
For the pragmatist, no metaphysical hypothesis is truer than another.   He who feels the
need of having one may choose according to
his purposes and tastes." [1]   But in spite of
Papini, most pragmatists (including Papini
himself) *have* a metaphysic; and certainly no
American or British pragmatist would take
seriously the suggestion one seems to get out
of the rather dogmatic article from which I
have just quoted — the suggestion, namely,
of an *Index Expurgatorius*, to be issued by
a pragmatic pope, proscribing all questions
which are not of interest to him.

It is disappointing indeed to come back
from our long search thus empty-handed.
But if we are to be honest with ourselves, I
think we must admit that pragmatism's

[1] " Introduzione al Pragmatismo," Leonardo, February,
1907, pp. 28–30.

much-vaunted method, if it is to save itself
from absurd dogmatism, really sifts down to
the following rather trifling rule: Never discuss a question which has absolutely no
interest and no meaning to any one. Pragmatism's insistence upon the concrete and its
warnings against logomachy, I confess, are
admirable. And its view of meaning as dependent on *some one's* experience seems
philosophically sound. But both of these
things are to be found in almost every school
of philosophy and are far too common to be
appropriated by any one group of thinkers
as their peculiar merit or message. And
when pragmatism attempts to go beyond
these somewhat commonplace precepts, it
lands in dogmatism and absurdity.

Meaning and method, however, are, after
all, but the beginning of pragmatism. Important as these are in judging it, its doctrine of truth is more vital still. It may be,
then, that here we shall find something both
unique and tenable, — a genuine and valuable contribution to philosophy and to

clear thinking. But "truth" is a large and
perplexing question (as you will soon see to
your sorrow), and the consideration of it
must therefore be postponed to the next
lecture.

LECTURE II

THE AMBIGUITY OF "TRUTH"

LECTURE II

THE AMBIGUITY OF "TRUTH"[1]

PRAGMATISM has been likened by one of its foremost exponents to the corridor of a hotel. It is a way of approach to a number of diverse but related philosophic doctrines, rather than itself a new philosophy. And yet, in spite of the perfect intellectual freedom and non-conformity of the pragmatists, all or nearly all of them would insist that there are two or three important articles of faith common to all pragmatist creeds; and that the most important of these is the new meaning which pragmatism has given to the word *truth*. This new theory of truth is by far the most fundamental and important doctrine yet proposed by the new movement. It gives the point of view

[1] Portions of this and the following lectures appeared in the *Jour. of Phil.*, Vol. IV, pp. 320–324, and Vol. V, pp. 122–131.

from which the pragmatist sees his world, it is the center from which most of his other doctrines take their start. It is, in fact, even more like the corridor of a hotel than pragmatism itself, — its doctrine of meaning being the front steps. To get at any of the other pragmatist doctrines one must first of all pass these. The question of truth, moreover, is even more important than that of meaning, and is, in fact, the most fundamental, the most crucial point to be met with in the whole pragmatic problem, and a thorough understanding of it is essential to all our subsequent studies. Pragmatism stands or falls with its conception of truth.

Before attempting an exposition of the new meaning assigned to this word, however, it may be well to remind you (what you undoubtedly know perfectly well) that ever since Pilate's time the word *truth* has been notoriously ambiguous. Stop half a dozen men in the street and ask them, What is truth? and you will probably get as many different answers. The number of *ways* in which the word truth may be *used* seems, however, to be reducible to three, and a clear understanding of these and of the distinctions between them is absolutely indispensable to any one who would thoroughly comprehend pragmatism. This lecture, therefore, will be devoted to an attempt to clear up this rather difficult subject, and to explain some of the different meanings given to the word truth — our exposition and criticism of the more technical pragmatist use of the word being reserved for the next lecture. The subject, I say, may prove difficult; yet I trust it will not be hopelessly so. For it is my firm belief that the difficulties which it usually presents are almost entirely due to a neglect of the distinctions referred to, and to a constant and unconscious confusion between the different senses of the word truth.

The three different ways in which the word truth is commonly used are, then, the

following: (1) as a synonym for "reality";
(2) as a synonym for known "fact" or
verified and accepted belief; (3) as the
relation or quality belonging to an "idea"
which makes it "*true*" — its *trueness*. We
shall now consider each of these in their
order.

The first of these uses is quite common
in popular speech. The word is thus em-
ployed as synonymous sometimes with the
whole of reality, more often with a part
only; namely, that rather indefinite part
which in popular discourses is referred to
as Infinite, Eternal, Changeless, etc. Nor
is the identification of truth with reality
confined to popular speech; philosophers
of the Platonic and Hegelian type — the
absolutists in general — have often a tendency in this direction. Truth is thus regarded as "objective," "systematic," independent of our human thinking, and as
really another name for ultimate reality.
This general position is maintained, for instance, by Mr. Bradley and Mr. Joachim.

Thus in a recent article[1] Mr. Bradley tells us that " Truth is the whole Universe realizing itself in one aspect." Truth and reality must be identical, for were there any difference between them, truth would fall short of reality and so fail to be true. Against this view of truth pragmatism — using especially the sword-like pen of Dr. Schiller, — has done magnificent battle, and has, in my opinion, come off with most of the spoils of war. It has shown the confusion which such a view brings into our terminology, its lack of self-consistency, and the almost inevitable skepticism consequent upon it, owing to its " dehumanizing " of truth.

In all this pragmatism is decidedly in the right; for the philosophic identification of truth with reality seems, to me at least, quite untenable, and the popular use of the word in this sense most unfortunate. Mr. Bradley himself has shown that truth " in passing over into reality " ceases to be mere truth

[1] "On Truth and Copying," *Mind*, April, 1907.

and that "truth at once is and is not reality."
In short, this kind of reasoning, so far from
what Professor Dewey calls the concrete
situation, is most unsatisfactory and inevitably develops its own destructive "dialectic."

Nor is the popular use of "truth" in the
sense of reality any more satisfactory, although not open to the same logical criticisms. Its tendency toward vagueness,
rhetoric, and a capital T ought to be enough
to condemn it in the eyes of all those who
would think clearly. To use the mildest of
epithets, it is at least exceedingly unfortunate, both because of its haziness and also
because the word truth is badly needed else-
where, — a remark which applies to both the
popular and the philosophic use of the word
referred to. The English language is none
too rich in clear-cut philosophic terms, and
it is most unwise and most conducive to
ambiguity to use up a good word like truth
on something for which we already have
another good word, namely reality. For, of
course, if "truth" is to mean everything, it

will end by meaning nothing. In its attack upon the identification of truth with reality, pragmatism has, therefore, done a genuine service to the cause of clear thinking.

The second general meaning commonly applied to the word truth is perfectly clear-cut, definite, and justifiable — its identifica-tion, namely, with *known fact*, with the true and more or less completely verified beliefs that go to make up the mass of human knowledge. That twice two is four, that the earth revolves upon its axis, that virtue is its own reward, — these we speak of as "truths." In like manner, we speak of the various "truths" of science or of the body of moral and religious "truths." Or we may go still further, and, combining all the general and important facts known to the race, we may speak of this whole as truth, — or even, if you like, as Truth. A capital letter is no serious danger if you keep your eyes open. Only we must remember that here as else-where eternal vigilance is the price of safety; and the history of philosophy shows many

examples of the inherent human tendency
toward worship manifesting itself in an
apotheosis of this very capital T. Thus it
has come about that the human element in
all the truth we know has often been quite
lost from sight. Now it may very well be that
there is an Absolute or Divine Mind, and that
in that Mind there exist all manner of truths
which have in them no human element. It is
far from my purpose to decry monism or absolutism. But certain it is that the only truths
we know or ever can know contain *ipso facto*
a human element, and that this element cannot be lightly despised. It is in the pointing
out of just this fact, in the emphasis laid upon
just this human side of human truth, that the
chief merit of pragmatism or humanism lies.
It may indeed be seriously questioned whether
the "intellectualists" in their treatment of
truth have so completely left out of account
its human side as they are accused of doing.
I know of few who maintain the existence
of "truth with no one thinking it," which
pragmatists often refer to as the type of

truth of the intellectualists.   There are, to be sure, a few English thinkers who hold to that doctrine.   But I should certainly challenge the assertion that this is the distinctive doctrine of the non-pragmatist and the consequent implication that in attacking it pragmatism has been quite original.   As a non-pragmatist I repudiate any such doctrine.   " Discarnate truth," truths which no one, not even an Absolute, thinks, like Platonic Ideas in an abstract empyrean, are as little to the taste of most non-pragmatists as to that of James, Schiller, and Dewey. And we have only sincere admiration for the brilliant exposition given by them of the contributions which we men make to our own truth.

In his admirable paper on " The Ambiguity of Truth," Dr. Schiller makes a useful distinction between those beliefs which have not yet been vindicated and those which have been proved true.   " If not all that claims truth is true, must we not distinguish this initial claim from whatever procedure subsequently justifies or validates? *Truth* therefore will become ambiguous. It will mean primarily a claim which may or may not turn out to be valid. It will mean, secondarily, such a claim *after* it has been tested and ratified, by processes which it behooves us to examine. In the first sense, as a claim, it will always have to be regarded with suspicion. For we shall not know whether it is really and fully true, and we shall tend to reserve this honorable predicate for what has victoriously sustained its claim."[1]   In other words, at least two things are essential, according to the pragmatist, for the definition of "a truth" in the full and exact sense of the word: (1) it shall be a claim which some one makes, a belief or judgment which some one holds; (2) it shall have been validated and verified as true.   A claim not yet verified is not yet a truth, insists the pragmatist.   And, here though we might indeed quarrel with him, we need not.   There is of course an obvious difference between a claim's

[1] "Studies in Humanism," pp. 144-145.

being true and its being known as true; and hence, if one cared to do so, one might very consistently maintain that a true claim is "a truth" even if not yet verified. Such an objection to the pragmatist's definition, however, would be largely verbal, and upon questions of terminology either side may well make concessions. It makes but little difference whether we call a claim which is true but unverified "a truth" or merely a true claim. And as it is my earnest desire not to be hypercritical but to go with the pragmatist just as far as possible, I shall agree to define "a truth" as a true claim that has been verified.[1]

[1] With this understanding of our terminology, therefore, the non-pragmatist need not and does not insist on unverifiable *truths*, though he does insist that there may be and doubtless are innumerable beliefs which are *true* though as yet unverified or even unverifiable. The failure to grasp this distinction is the cause of Dr. Schiller's caricature of the non-pragmatist position. Cf. his review of Professor James's book in *Mind*, Vol. XVI, p. 600. The non-pragmatist is not driven to assert "unknowables" in any other sense than that there doubtless are many things in heaven and earth that we can never know — an assertion which, I suppose, pragmatism would hardly deny.

So much being agreed and understood, let us now take a brief survey of the pragmatist's admirable description of the way our truths originate and grow.   In doing so, however, let me remind you of the importance of keeping in mind constantly that here there is as yet no question of the *trueness* of a claim or belief. The distinction between "a truth" and the trueness of that truth must never be lost from sight.

A large part of the writings of the three leading pragmatists is taken up with admirable psychological descriptions of "the making of truth."   For being part of the content of our minds, our truths have a natural history, and the general course of their development may be clearly traced.   Each truth which you or I possess originates and grows within a perfectly concrete situation and is due to perfectly definite conditions. Our beliefs are intellectual tools which serve us in more or less useful ways.   The process by which they get themselves verified and thus cease to be mere claims and become truths, the

application of these "truths," and the modi-
fications they undergo, — all this can be
traced within the stream of consciousness as
concrete psychic fact. If now we ask ourselves how, more in detail, our claims are
verified and proved true, we find that, if the
answer must be given in a single phrase, the
best way to describe what happens is to say
that those claims are accepted as truths which
work, which *are useful*, which combine harmoniously with our previously accepted
truths. By their fruits ye shall know them.
As we never can get outside of our own experience and compare our truths with anything beyond them, the best if not the only
test left us by which we may separate the
sheep from the goats, the potential truths
from the invalid claims, is to see which of
several possible combinations of claims is the
most self-consistent and inclusive; or, if it be
a question of a single claim, to observe how
well it works, how far it aids in harmonizing all our experience. Thus when a jury is
weighing the two possible views of the evi-

dence presented respectively by the defense
and by the prosecution, what it is really
about is an endeavor to see which view is
most consistent with itself and which, at the
same time, is able to interpret and harmonize
the largest number of individual claims.   Or
when a scientist is trying to decide whether
an hypothesis is true, his test is again the
question, How useful is it in harmonizing all
the accepted facts and leading the mind out
of its state of uncertainty to a feeling of in-
ner peace and intellectual satisfaction? The
truth is that which works best, and that which
works best is the truth.

Successful working is therefore the tag or
ear-mark by which we distinguish the true
idea.   But, as you doubtless perceive, this
only leads us to the more fundamental and
difficult question as to what we mean by the
idea's being true, the question of the nature
of the thing tagged or marked.   For it is
clear enough that there is a difference between a thing and its tag, — between an
object and the sign which proves to us the

presence of that object. Although we have
been informed how to tell a true idea when
we happen upon one, we must still ask what
is meant by the truth of the idea, what it is
that the sign of it signifies. The distinction
between a thing and the evidence of it, between an object and its tag, is doubtless plain
as day to you all; but as the distinction is an
extremely important one, and as it is often
overlooked, I shall, in good pragmatist fashion, seek a concrete illustration of it from a
realm of practical life far removed from the
abstractions of philosophy. Let us, for example, suppose that Mennen's face is, as he
says, upon every box of toilet powder made
by him. The presence of his face would,
then, be a good test by which to determine
whether in any given instance we have the
genuine article or not. But the important
thing about the powder, after all, is its own
nature and make-up rather than the pretty
picture associated with it; and we should
hardly say that the contents of the box is
what it is *because* its cover bears the image

of Mennen's never-to-be-forgotten face.   If a
pupil asks his teacher about a triangle, the
latter may refer him to page 52 of Loomis's
Geometry and page 63 of Wentworth's for a
diagram, and the pupil may learn to distinguish a triangle from a square in this way.
But even if the triangle were figured on no
other pages than these, one would not *define*
triangle as "the figure on pages 52 and 63,"
nor give this as the *meaning* of the term.
In other words, the meaning or nature of a
material, a quality, a relation, is one thing;
the sign by which you make sure of its presence is another.   And, in like manner (to
return to the question that immediately concerns us), the ear-mark by which we have
now learned to tell a true idea from a false
one does not answer the further question,
what we mean by its being true.   Doubtless
ideas are *proved* true by their consequences,
as the pragmatists say; but when we prove
them true, what are we proving?   What is it
that such a process of verification verifies?
A mere psychological description of what

happens within our experience is obviously here quite insufficient. And this brings us to the third use of the word *truth*, the *trueness* of a belief. To put it tersely, then, what do we mean when we say that an idea is true?

To this question there are certainly two and possibly several quite distinct answers. And it will throw light on the real meaning of the answer which pragmatism gives if we first consider the answer which pragmatism rejects, — the interpretation, namely, given by "common sense," or "intellectualism," or "realism" (as you like). This interpretation commonly goes under the name of the "correspondence theory," and runs in brief somewhat as follows: The truth relation, or the quality of *trueness*, is neither a part of our thought or experience, nor a part of the other reality to which our thought refers, but is rather a relation between our thought and its chosen object, between our idea or judgment and the thing which it means. And this relation is simply one of *correspondence*.

F

A caricature of the theory frequently set up by its opponents maintains that *correspondence* must mean *copying*, and that the thought which thus "copies" reality is a sort of photograph of the original; that we have *pictures* of things in our heads, and that if the pictures are good pictures we have truth.

Now the upholder of the correspondence theory will agree with his critics that the copy theory as thus described would deserve all the uncomplimentary epithets they are so able in devising for it. Such a theory would be both bad psychology and bad epistemology. For, in the first place, it is obvious that the great majority of all those thoughts which can be called either true or false are not pictures; and if they were, it is hard to see how their simply being like external things could make them true. A billiard ball is not *true*, no matter how much it may resemble another billiard ball. Two pains are not true, though they be as like as two peas. Whatever truth may be, it is at any rate something more than chance resemblance. The knowing thought must *mean* its object, must choose and adopt it, and once it has done so no copying will be necessary.

The real common-sense theory, as I understand it, may then be stated as follows: "Truth," or the relation of "correspondence," means, not copying, but merely this simple thing, that *the object of which one is thinking is as one thinks it.* Or, to put the same thing in other words, the truth or trueness of an idea is its *conformity to fact.*

It would seem, oddly enough, that this very obvious and natural explanation of the meaning of the truth relation is the one thing in the universe which is capable of bringing together the absolutist and the pragmatist. Deadly enemies at every other point, they stand manfully shoulder to shoulder in attacking the correspondence theory. Whatever else truth may mean, they are agreed it shall not mean this. For Mr. Bradley it is far too simple, and for Professor James, apparently, it is not simple enough. In commenting upon the formulation of the doctrine just given (that the object of which one is thinking is as one thinks it), Professor James finds the word "*as*" to be "anything but simple." "What it most immediately suggests," he continues, "is that the idea should be *like* the object; but most of our ideas, being abstract concepts, bear almost no resemblance to their objects. . . . I now formally ask . . . what this 'as'ness in itself consists in — for it seems to me that it ought to consist in something assignable and describable and not remain a pure mystery."[1]

Paulsen has somewhere remarked that "the absurd has this advantage in common with truth, that it cannot be refuted." And it might be added that the most ultimately simple expression of the commonest fact has this disadvantage in common with the self-contradictory, that it cannot be explained. As Dr. Ewer has pointed out in connection with this very question of Professor James's, "We recognize similar questions about in-

[1] "Professor Pratt on Truth," *Jour. of Phil.*, Vol. IV, pp. 466–467.

dubitable facts that have no answer: 'How
can a body move?' 'How can a body
exclude other bodies from the space it
occupies?' 'How can one event follow
another?' . . . To them no answers can
be given which do not contain the very
ideas of motion, temporal succession, etc.,
that are under fire. Details and accessories
of the process may be elucidated, but the
essential character is implied throughout."[1]
In short, it is the very simplicity of the relation between our thought and the thing
of which we are thinking that makes it in-
capable of reduction to simpler terms. It
may be a "pure mystery" no doubt; but if
so, then I ask in turn that something be
named me which is not a mystery. And
even if the nature of the case permitted my
accepting Professor James's challenge and
naming something else which "this 'as 'ness
in itself *consists* in," he could again ask the
same question concerning this new thing,
and so *ad infinitum.*

[1] "The Anti-realistic 'How?'" *Jour. of Phil.*, Vol. IV,
p. 631.

But though I cannot analyze an ultimately simple relation into its parts and tell what 'as 'ness consists in, it will, I feel sure, clear up the matter completely to the non-pragmatic reader if I apply the correspondence theory of truth to a concrete and very commonplace example. John, let us say, thinks Peter has a toothache; the object of John's thought is Peter's present experience; and as a fact Peter *has* a toothache. And John's thought is true, according to the correspondence theory, *because its object is as he thinks it.* That is what constitutes it true, that is the meaning of its trueness. And I confess it is impossible for me to see how anything could be simpler than this. To torture it into some sort of mysterious and crude " copy theory," and to insist upon further simplification and demand what 'as 'ness consists in, seems to me a manufacture of unnecessary difficulties. At any rate, if this explanation of the meaning of " *true* " be not simple and clear, I despair of ever making anything clear to philosophers.

But lack of simplicity is not the only charge brought against the correspondence theory by pragmatism. Leaving this question to Professor James, Dr. Schiller attacks it in two other quarters. In the first place he tells us that this view of truth " speedily leads us to a hopeless *impasse* once the question is raised — How are we to know whether our 'truth' 'corresponds' or 'agrees' with its real object ? For to decide this question must we not be able to compare 'thought' and 'reality,' and to contemplate each apart from the other ? This, however, seems impossible. 'Thought' and 'reality' cannot be got apart, and consequently the doctrine of their 'correspondence' has in the end no meaning. We are not aware of any reality except by its representation in our 'thought' and *per contra*, the whole meaning of 'thought' resides ultimately in its reference to 'reality.'" [1]

By the above, Dr. Schiller can hardly mean simply that all reality is some form

[1] " Humanism," pp. 45–46.

of experience, for there is, of course, nothing
to prevent two independent experiences —
my thought and my neighbor's experience,
for instance — from corresponding (in the
sense defined above). More probably Dr.
Schiller means that we can never get immediately at any reality but our own thought
or experience, that we can never get outside
of our own minds, and that every part of
reality which is to be directly grasped by
us must become part of our own experience;
and that, hence, we are not able to compare
and contemplate thought and reality apart
from each other. If I am right in this interpretation, then by saying, "Thought and
reality cannot be got apart," he means that
we cannot get them apart. Certainly this
is far from proving that they cannot *be* apart
and correspond, and that the "doctrine of
their correspondence has in the end no
meaning." Its meaning is perfectly obvious — at least to every one whose eyes are
not afflicted with pragmatic cataracts. But,
to make it concrete, let us again take an ex-

ample. I am thinking, let us say, that my friend B is in Constantinople. Let us say, too, that though I am and remain without any experience of Constantinople, my friend B actually *is* there. Surely thought and reality are here "apart" — though it remains a fact that they cannot "be got apart," *i.e.* by any individual human experience. Dr. Schiller's argument would therefore seem to prove nothing more than that if truth consists in correspondence, it must transcend the individual human mind — it must be a relation such that only one of its terms is in the individual's experience; which is exactly what the upholders of the theory in question have always maintained.

Dr. Schiller has, however, another objection to the doctrine of correspondence, — namely, that if truth consists in this relation we can never know whether in any given case the correspondence holds or not; we shall never be able to tell whether a given thought is true.

In answer to this an upholder of the old

theory might well respond: "What of it? Suppose this so; would that make the nature and meaning of truth as defined inconsistent or impossible?" And here we come upon a point of considerable importance — the question, namely, whether my thought can be true if I do not know it to be true. On this the pragmatists seem to be divided. Sometimes they admit that such a thought would be true,[1] sometimes they avoid the issue,[2] and sometimes they flatly deny the possibility.[3] This latter position seems to rest upon a failure to distinguish between "a truth," and the truth relation, the quality of trueness or of being true. Granted that a "claim" must be verified to become "a truth," does it follow that there are no such things as true though unverified claims? Surely the pragmatist would hesitate to call all such claims false. And it is rather hard to see how they could be *neither* true *nor* false, though simple enough to understand that (according to the useful though arbitrary

[1] *E.g.* James.   [2] *E.g.* Schiller.   [3] *E.g.* Dewey and Schiller.

definition) they are as yet neither "truths" nor falsehoods.   It is therefore one thing to have a true idea or make a valid claim, and quite another to know that the idea is true or the claim valid.   Hence Dr. Schiller's assertion that we cannot find out whether our thought is true is utterly irrelevant to the question what we *mean* by its being true. The test of truth is one thing; the nature or meaning of truth quite another.

But it is not the case that on the correspondence theory we cannot tell whether a thought is true.   To be sure, the shadow of a very theoretical doubt may always be left us in all matters outside of our immediate here and now.   The proofs that my friend B is in Constantinople may be false, I may be dreaming, this may be a solipsistic world, etc.   But such a doubt is so exceedingly theoretical that it ought to have no terrors for any man — least of all for a pragmatist.   If, however, his pragmatic conscience is still unaccountably troubled by so purely theoretic and academic a question, let him tell us how his theory of truth avoids the difficulty. And to show that it is here no better off than the much-reviled correspondence theory, I need surely do no more than summon Professor James as my witness. For in dealing with this very question he writes, "If there is to be truth, both realities and beliefs about them must conspire to make it; but whether there ever is such a thing, or how any one can be sure that his own beliefs possess it, pragmatism never pretends to determine."[1] — The fact is, as a practical matter, much the same *tests* of truth hold, no matter what your theory. If you grant that it is at all possible for me to prove that Boston is in Massachusetts, that Cæsar lived before Napoleon, that my friend B is in Constantinople, then on the correspondence theory as well as on any other I can know that my thought is true.

This being the case, it is really hard to see why pragmatism has rejected it. The

---

[1] "The Pragmatist Account of Truth," *Phil. Rev.*, Vol. XVII, p. 8.

correspondence view of truth is perfectly consistent with the humanistic attitude toward
truth and the making of truth. It not only
admits but insists that our human thought
is indispensable to the truth relation, and that
without it such a relation could not exist. It
is essentially realistic (which ought to please
pragmatism, for pragmatism at least pretends
to be realistic), and it combines more naturally and easily with empiricism than with
rationalism. And it is glad to admit that
the way our ideas "work" in the broad sense
is one of the most important tests of their
being true. In spite of all this, however,
the leading pragmatists, one and all, refuse
to accept the theory, considering it either
quite inadequate or flatly meaningless and
false.

This is a fact which I wish especially to
emphasize. One frequently gets the impression from the writings of the pragmatists
that all they have done is innocently to call
attention to an obvious characteristic of the
truth relation, which their opponents have

thereupon unaccountably and wickedly denied, and that the latter are, therefore, at
all points the aggressors. As a fact, the
exact opposite of this is the case. No one,
so far as I know, denies the usefulness of
truth nor the value of successful working as
verification of the true idea. And if the
pragmatists had been satisfied with pointing
this out and with their further (rather confusing and unwarranted) endeavor to identify
the word " truth " with " successful working,"
and had stopped there, no one would have
thought it worth while to dispute with them
over a matter which would obviously have
been one of terminology only. But they
have not stopped there; and the question at
issue is really one of fundamental importance
to clear thinking for the reason that the
pragmatists have not only appropriated the
word truth to their own meaning, but also
insist that the meaning which most other
philosophers have given to the word is no
meaning at all. It is they, therefore, rather
than the non-pragmatists, who are the real

aggressors and who refuse, rather intoler-
antly, to recognize the existence of any other
relation or characteristic of a true idea besides
that which they themselves designate by the
word truth. In one of his latest contributions to the subject, Professor James says of
the correspondence theory: "Surely this is
not a counter-theory of truth to ours. It is
the renunciation of all articulate theory. It
is but a claim to the right to *call* certain
ideas true *anyhow;* and this is what I meant
by saying that the anti-pragmatists offer us
no real alternative, and that our account is
literally the only positive theory extant."[1]
Unconditional surrender, in other words, is
the only terms pragmatism will offer its
opponents; and the non-pragmatist, no matter how peaceable his disposition, is thus
forced to take up arms in very self-defense.
This categorical denial by the pragmatists
that there is any meaning in the correspondence theory must be kept constantly in mind

[1] Review of Hébert's "Le Pragmatisme," *Jour. of Phil.*,
Vol. V, p. 692.

in our attempt to understand the theory (or theories?) of the truth relation which they propose in its place. This, however, is a large question, and we must postpone consideration of it to the next lecture.

LECTURE III

THE PRAGMATIC VIEW OF THE TRUTH RELATION

LECTURE III

THE PRAGMATIC VIEW OF THE TRUTH
RELATION

No one can fully grasp the pragmatic meaning of the truth relation without first understanding the pragmatic view of the nature of "a truth" or verified human claim discussed in the last lecture. And the reason is, as I shall try to show, that the former grows out of the latter and is the result of a complete confusion between the two uses of the word truth. It is impossible to read half a dozen pages of pragmatist writing on this subject without coming upon at least one, and usually many, instances of utter failure to distinguish between "truth" as known fact, or mental possession, and "truth" as trueness or that quality or relation characterizing a true idea which makes it *true*. I trust that by this time you all

are clear on this distinction and appreciate
its importance. For it is from a failure to
make this distinction that pragmatism has
fallen into the pitiful and unnecessary difficulties, inconsistencies, and impossible situations, which I shall try to point out.

There are several roads by which pragmatism seems to have moved from its position
on the nature of "a truth" to the meaning
it has given to the truth relation. Of these
I shall point out two. (1) We have noted
the emphasis placed by pragmatists upon
the concrete, psychological nature of our
human truths. These do not, they insist,
dwell apart in a Platonic realm ; they are all
of them concrete mental facts, they are of
such stuff as dreams and feelings and sensations are made of. To banish the abstract
from philosophy so far as possible and to substitute for it the individual concrete in the
interests of clear thinking has been one of
the great and excellent aims of pragmatism.
What more natural, therefore, than to use
the same concrete method in dealing with

the further question of the *trueness* of ideas? If truth in this sense be a relation, it must, insists the pragmatist, be a concrete relation. In fact, long before pragmatism was heard of Professor James sought in his " Principles of Psychology " to interpret every relation concretely so far as possible.[1] This principle applied to the truth relation makes it no mere correspondence as defined above, but rather the chain or succession of things or events or experiences that are to be found either between an idea and its object or between a judgment and its vindication. Not only, therefore, is "a truth " concrete; pragmatism insists that its *trueness* also shall be a concrete thing or group of things. It is this chain of intermediating things or experiences that not only proves it true but also *makes* it true, and *constitutes its truth*. The truth relation is therefore not " saltatory " but "ambulatory "[2] — it consists not in the mere fact that our object is there as we think it, but

[1] See especially Vol. I, pp. 243 ff.; Vol. II, pp. 148 ff.

[2] " A Word more about Truth," *Jour. of Phil.*, Vol. IV, pp. 396 f.

in the actual experiential process of getting at
it or as near it as may be. " The links of experience sequent upon an idea, which mediate
between it and reality, form and, for the pragmatist, indeed, *are* the *concrete* relation of
truth that may obtain between the idea and
that reality. They, he says, are all that we
mean when we speak of the idea 'pointing'
to the reality, 'fitting' it, 'corresponding'
with it or 'agreeing' with it, — they and
other similar mediating trains of verification. Such mediating events *make* the idea
'true.' The idea itself, if it exists at all, is
also a concrete event; so that pragmatism
insists that truth in the singular is only a
collective name for truths in the plural,
these consisting always of series of definite
events."[1]   I shall not at this point offer any
criticism of this view that *trueness* is a collective name for concrete psychic *truths*, being
concerned here merely in pointing out this
first mode of transition from the latter to the
former.

[1] " The Pragmatist Account of Truth," *Phil. Rev.*, Vol.
XVII, p. 11.

(2) Another road which has led the pragmatist to the same result starts from the
view already dealt with that our "truths"
are made, that they begin as claims and are
verified within our experience, and that the
test of their verity is their working, their
consequences, their application.   Now the
pragmatist contention that a claim must be
verified in order to become "a truth" is
neither novel nor open to any serious criticism; but the pragmatist takes it for granted
that once this is admitted it follows that the
claim is *made true* by being verified and that
its trueness consists in its verification.
Verification thereby ceases to be the process of *proving* an idea to be true and
becomes the process of *making* it true.
"Truths are logical values," says Dr. Schiller; and he adds, "It directly follows from
this definition of truth that all 'truths'
must be verified to be properly true. . . .
To become really true it has to be tested,
and it is tested by being applied. . . . The
truth of an assertion depends upon its appli-

cation. . . .   In short, truths must be used to
become true, and (in the end) to stay true." [1]
Just how " it directly follows " " that all
truths must be verified to be properly true "
may not seem so obvious to us as it does to
Dr. Schiller; for the premise to such a conclusion must evidently be that no belief can
be true unless it is known to be true, and
the logical consequence is, of course, that
there are no such things as true but unverified beliefs, and that before a belief is verified it is either false or else neither true nor
false.

Let me sum up this rather difficult point
in a few words. We all agree that verification is essential to the making of a claim into a truth; but the pragmatist draws from
this the conclusion that the *truth* (*trueness*)
of the claim depends on and consists in its
verification. This, I maintain, is a flagrant
case of using the word *truth* in two perfectly distinct senses as if it meant the same
thing both times and as if it had but one

[1] " Studies in Humanism," pp. 7–9.

meaning. It is a confusion between a "truth" and "trueness," — a fallacy from which flow, as will be seen, the most serious consequences.

Or, to put the same thing in another light, the claim being *proved* true by its working, by its consequences, it is said to be *made* true (notice, not made "a truth" but made *true*) by these consequences. Its trueness thus consists in these consequences. "The truth (validity) of a truth (claim)," says Schiller, "is tested and established by the value of its consequences."[2] This sentence is perfectly harmless, but the pragmatist does not stop here. From it he deduces the rather amazing conclusion that since its usefulness proves it true, its trueness consists in its being useful. The test of truth and the meaning of truth are thus completely identified.

So much for pragmatism's roads of approach to its final view of the truth relation. And now, lest I should unwittingly misrep-

[1] "Studies in Humanism," p. 160.

resent that view, let the three great pragmatists speak for it: —

Professor James: "Theoretical truth is
no relation between our mind and the archetypal reality. It falls *within* the mind, being the accord of some of its processes and
objects with other processes and objects."[1]
"Truth happens to an idea. It becomes
true, is made true by events. Its verity *is*
in fact an event, a process; the process,
namely, of its verifying itself, its veri-*fication*.
Its validity is the process of its valid-*ation*."[2]
"The truth of our beliefs consists in general
in their giving satisfaction."[3] "The links
of experience sequent upon an idea, which
mediate between it and a reality, form, and
for the pragmatist, indeed, *are* the *concrete* relation of truth. . . . Such mediating events
make the idea true."[4] "The truth relation
is a definitely experienceable relation. . . .
The relation to its object that makes an idea

[1] "Humanism and Truth once More," *Mind*, Vol. XIV,
p. 198.   [2] "Pragmatism," p. 201.
[3] "The Pragmatist Account of Truth," *Phil. Rev.*, Vol.
XVII, p. 5.   [4] *Ibid.*, p. 11.

true in any given instance is, we say, embodied in intermediate details of reality which lead towards the object, which vary in every instance, and which in every instance can be concretely traced. The chain of workings which an idea sets up *is* the opinion's truth, falsity, or irrelevancy, as the case may be. . . . These 'workings' differ in every single instance, they never transcend experience, they consist of particulars, mental or sensible, and they admit of concrete description in every individual case. Pragmatists are unable to see what you can possibly *mean* by calling an idea true, unless you mean that between it as a *terminus a quo* in some one's mind and some particular reality as a *terminus ad quem*, such concrete workings do or may intervene. Their direction constitutes the idea's reference to that reality, their satisfactoriness constitutes its adaptation thereto, and the two things together constitute the 'truth' of the idea for its possessor."[1]

---

[1] Hébert's "Le Pragmatisme," *Jour. of Phil.*, Vol. V, pp. 691–692.

Dr. Schiller: Truth is "a function of our intellectual activity or a manipulation of our objects which turns out to be useful."[1] While some truths may be conceived as correspondences or agreements, this is only on condition " that these processes remain strictly *immanent* in *human* knowing." They are " valuable and serviceable cross-references which obtain *within* our experience."[2] " All truths must be verified to be properly true."[3] " If truth could win no recognition, it would so far not work, and so fail to be true."[4]

Professor Dewey: " Truth is an *experienced*[5] relation of characteristic quality of things, and it has no meaning outside of such [experienced] relation."[6] " From this [the pragmatic] point of view verification and truth are two names for the same thing."

[1] " Humanism," p. 61.

[2] " Mr. Bradley's Theory of Truth," *Mind*, Vol. XVI, p. 404.　　　　　[3] " Studies in Humanism," p. 8.

[4] *Ibid.*, p. 70.　　　　[5] Italics mine.

[6] " The Experimental Theory of Knowledge," *Mind*, Vol. XV, p. 305.

As an illustration, Professor Dewey cites an idea that a certain noise comes from a street car; this idea being investigated and verified *becomes* true. Had it not been verified it never would have been true, — even if as a fact the noise *had* really come from the car. To say that the idea was true before it was verified is, he insists, either tautologous ("being just a restatement of the fact that the idea has, as a matter of fact, worked successfully"), or else, in any other sense, it is simply false. Exactly speaking, the idea is not true till it works out, for its working and its truth are identical. "What the experimentalist means is that the effective working of the idea and its truth are one and the same thing — this working being neither the cause nor the evidence of truth but its nature."[1]

To give a fair presentation of the pragmatist view of truth, however, I must add that throughout the writings of Professor James — and more especially in what he

---

[1] "Reality and the Criterion of Truth for Ideas," *Mind*, Vol. XVI, pp. 335–337.

has published since the appearance of his
" Pragmatism " — there runs, parallel with
the view expressed above, a different and
decidedly less radical description of the nature of the truth relation.[1] Thus *verifiability*
is often spoken of as being *as good as verification.* And in the *Journal of Philosophy*
for August 15, 1907, he writes, " Truth is
essentially a relation between two things, an
idea, on the one hand, and a reality outside
of the idea, on the other. This relation, like
all relations, has its *fundamentum*, namely
the matrix of experiential circumstance, psychological as well as physical, in which the
correlated terms are found embedded. . . .
What *constitutes the relation* known as truth,
I now say, is just the *existence in the empirical world of this fundamentum* of circumstance surrounding object and idea and ready

[1] I should add, however, that in his latest treatment of the
subject, namely in his review of Hébert's recent book on
Pragmatism, Professor James seems to have returned part
way to the more radical view, while still maintaining the
reality and independence of the object. See the *Jour. of
Phil.* for December 3, 1908.

to be either short-circuited or traversed at full length. So long as it *exists* and a satis- factory passage through it between the object and the idea is *possible*, that idea will both *be* true, and will *have been* true of that object, whether fully developed verification has taken place or not. The nature and place and affinities of the object, of course, play as vital a part in making the particular passage possible as do the nature and associ- ative tendencies of the idea; so that the notion that truth could fall altogether inside of the thinker's experience and be something purely psychological is absurd." And in a more recent article,[1] while still maintaining that the truth relation must be a chain of "concrete" links, he comes still closer to the correspondence theory. " The pragmatizing epistemologist posits a reality and a mind with ideas. What now, he asks, can make those ideas true of that reality? Ordinary epistemology contents itself with the vague

[1] " The Pragmatist Account of Truth," *Phil. Rev.*, Vol XVII, pp. 1-17.

statement that the ideas must 'correspond'
or 'agree'; the pragmatist insists upon being
more concrete and asks what such agreement
may mean in detail. He finds first that the
ideas must point to or lead towards *that*
reality and no other, and then that the point-
ings and leadings must yield satisfaction as
their result." " The pragmatist calls satisfactions indispensable for truth-building, but ex-
pressly calls them insufficient unless reality
be also incidentally led to. If the reality he
assumed were canceled from his universe of
discourse, he would straightway give the
name of falsehoods to the beliefs remaining
in spite of all their satisfactoriness. For him,
as for his critic, there can be no truth if there
is nothing to be true about. Ideas are so
much flat psychological surface unless some
mirrored matter gives them cognitive luster."
" Ideas are practically useful which we can
verify by the sum total of all their leadings,
and the reality of whose objects may thus be
considered established beyond doubt. That
these ideas should be true in advance of and

apart from their utility, that, in other words, their objects should be really there, is the very condition of their having that kind of utility." And even in his " Pragmatism" Professor James in one place writes, "When new experiences lead to retrospective judgments, using the past tense, what these judgments utter *was* true, even though no past thinker had been led there."[1]

How far Dr. Schiller goes with Professor James in his modified view of truth, I am unable to say. Professor James insists that he and Schiller agree absolutely on the subject.[2] Yet it is certainly very difficult to find in any of Dr. Schiller's writings anything comparable in explicitness to the expressions just quoted from Professor James. And Professor Dewey certainly stands firmly on the expressions quoted from him and remains always consistently radical.

After listening to the quotations I have just read you from the three leading prag-

[1] p. 223.
[2] See his review of Hébert's " Le Pragmatisme," in the *Jour. of Phil.*, Vol. V, pp. 693-694.

H

matists, you may understand why the critics
of pragmatism have been so constantly —
and justly! — accused of misunderstanding
it.

And I am free to confess that it is beyond
my power to formulate, on the basis of what
the pragmatists have written, a single consistent and harmonious pragmatic doctrine
concerning the nature of the truth relation.
The best I can do for pragmatism is to make
two doctrines of truth out of the expressions
quoted above; and, indeed, it must be evident
to you all that we have here two quite distinct views — one radical and one somewhat
modified — as to the meaning of truth. The
former of these holds that truth is the process of verification which goes on within
experience; that it consists in the successful
working of the idea, in the concrete steps
within consciousness that lead from the
unverified claim to the full and satisfying
assurance of its "goodness." The modified
view, on the other hand, maintains that there
are two factors which go to make up the

trueness of an idea: namely, (1) the concrete
steps of its leading and the subjective satisfactions resulting (as described by the radical
view); and also (2) the actual presence in
reality of the object which the idea means.
Let us note a little more in detail three of
the most important differences between these
two views.

(1) The most obvious difference is the
recognition found in the more moderate view
that it is indispensable for the trueness of an
idea that its object should really " be there." [1]
Truth thus ceases to be " wholly within our
experience," or " an experienced relation,"
and becomes instead a relation which completely transcends (or may transcend) any
single finite experience. It is not merely
a " process " nor a felt "leading" from one
part of our experience to another. It is no
more psychical than physical in its nature.
It is a relation between an idea and a reality

[1] Numerous expressions of the moderate pragmatist show
that by the object's being really "there" he means not only
that the object exists but that it exists independently of the
individual's experience, and (at times) outside of it.

which may be "beyond the direct experience of the particular cognizer,"[1] a relation which, apparently, no one short of a Roycean Absolute need ever experience. It must be evident to all how completely this differs from the radical view which takes no note of any reality outside the individual's experience as essential to truth, and which makes truth wholly a process within experience. And this brings us to the second difference between the two theories.

(2) Since the modified view of truth recognizes an outer reality as relevant and essential, it can and does maintain that an idea may be true before it is verified, whereas the radical view insists that truth consists in the actual process of verification, and that, hence, the idea is not true till so proved. Thus we have here another case of flat contradiction, Professor Dewey saying that the idea is not true before verified, and Professor James saying that it is. A less obvious but equally

---

[1] Professor James in the *Jour. of Phil.*, Vol. IV, p. 403, note.

important phase of this same disagreement is the question of verifiability. Professor Dewey and the left wing maintain, as has been seen, that actual verification is essential to truth; Professor James and the right wing maintain that verifiability is quite sufficient; while the center, under both Dr. Schiller and Professor James, insists that after all there isn't any real difference between the meanings of these two words. Whether there is such a difference or not, I must leave to your judgment. For my own part, I had always supposed there was the same difference as that between mere possibility and the concrete process of making the possibility an actuality; and I had also thought that this was a real difference. Columbus's idea that he could cross the Atlantic was merely verifiable so long as he stayed in Spain, and this its quality of verifiability (which it *already* possessed while he was still in Spain), had always seemed to me quite a different thing from the concrete steps of getting ships, manning them, hoisting anchor and raising sail and all the other links in the chain of actual verification. And it must, I think, be evident to all who are not pragmatists that it is one thing to say the full process of verification is essential to truth and a very different thing to say that verifiability alone is essential. For verifiability is not a process nor a succession of events in time, it is not included within any one's experience, but is a general condition or set of conditions which transcends every single finite experience. It is not a felt "leading," it is not a "form of the good," nor a "satisfactory working," nor any other experience or experience-process. It is, if you like, the *possibility* of these, but it is not these. It is a totality of relations which are not, and will never be, within any finite experience. It is a present condition of the idea, not something that "happens to" it. It is not "made"; it is already there. It is immeasurably more harmonious with the correspondence theory of truth than with that of radical pragmatism. The harmony which Dr. Schiller has brought about be-

tween verification and verifiability is of the
same sort that usually obtains between the
lion and the lamb when they lie down together. "It is," he tells us, "impossible to
separate verifiability from verification — the
potentiality does not exist apart from the actuality from which it is an *ex post facto* inference. A claim to truth, therefore, can
only be regarded as verifiable on the strength
of past experiences of verifications, and a
'verifiable' truth which is *never* verified is
really unverifiable."[1] It would seem, thus,
that the reason why verification and verifiability cannot be separated is the same that
makes it impossible to separate the lion and
the lamb after they have lain down together.
It is, therefore, obvious why Dr. Schiller insists that there is no difference between the
two; to his pragmatic mind there really is

[1] "Ultima Ratio?" *Jour. of Phil.*, Vol. IV, p. 493, note.
The non-pragmatist, of course, agrees with Schiller that a potentiality cannot exist apart from an actuality, but he insists
that the actuality which makes an idea verifiable is not actual
verification, but the existing condition of relevant reality, the
nature of the fact in question and the idea's conformity to
that fact.

no such thing as verifiability, it having been completely swallowed by verification. All of which is new evidence of the great difference between the view that considers mere verifiability without verification sufficient for truth and that which insists that actual verification is essential.

(3) The third difference between the left and right wings of pragmatism is hardly more than a variant on the second, and yet deserves especial notice. It is, namely, concerned with the question of the " successful working," or the "consequences," of an idea. Radical pragmatism maintains that these not only prove the idea true, but *make* it true and *constitute its truth*. Modified pragmatism denies the latter statement. Professor Dewey says, " The effective working of the idea and its truth are one and the same thing — this working being neither the cause nor the evidence of truth but its nature." Professor James says, " That these ideas (*i.e.* useful ideas) should be true in advance of and apart from their utility, that, in other

words, their objects should be really there, is the very condition of their having that kind of utility." In other words, to put it briefly, the left wing of pragmatism maintains that ideas are true because they are useful; the right wing maintains that they are useful because they are true.

Let us now examine more in detail this modified form of the pragmatic doctrine. In the first place, it is obvious that this is an attempt to steer a middle course between radical pragmatism and the old correspondence theory. It has sought for a combination of pragmatism and common sense as a sort of golden mean. The result has been, on the one hand, that it has avoided some of the difficult positions of the radical form; but, on the other hand, it is questionable whether it has not sought to reconcile several things which are quite irreconcilable. It would seem to be trying that notoriously difficult feat of eating one's cake and keeping it too. Thus it is hard to see how "satisfactions" and the concrete "links of

experience" are "indispensable" to truth, if
at the same time an idea can be true in advance of and apart from these satisfactions
and links of experience.

The modified pragmatist view would
therefore seem to be open to two different
interpretations, according to which of its
two seemingly inconsistent factors one
chooses to emphasize as the essential part.
If one emphasizes the assertion that the
idea is true before it is verified, that its
truth consists just in the existence of the
relation between it and its object even if
this be "short-circuited," and that it is its
truth that makes it useful rather than its
usefulness that makes it true, it is indeed
no longer subject to criticism, because it
has simply turned into the old correspondence theory under a new name. All that
was distinctive in it has evaporated, and all
that remains is the name "pragmatic" —
like the grin on the face of Alice's Cheshire
cat after the face of the cat had faded
away. But if, on the other hand, we choose

to say that the indispensability of the satisfactions and of the concrete links of experience forms the essential part of the doctrine, then we shall have avoided the frying pan, indeed, but only to fall dangerously near the fire. There will, of course, still be this difference between moderate and radical pragmatism : that for the former the object must really " be there " and that the satisfactions, etc., though indispensable, will not be sufficient. Yet, if these satisfactions are really indispensable, a belief which is verifiable but not yet verified is not true. My idea that my friend is in Constantinople will not be a true idea (even if as a fact he is there) until I have actually gone through the links of concrete experience which verify it and actually *have* the satisfactions which witness to its truth. Truth and the test of truth will thus still be largely confused; the proof of a proposition will form at least a part of its trueness. This doctrine, therefore, though differing in some details from the radical

pragmatism of Professor Dewey, will still
be subject to most of the criticisms to which
the latter view (as Professor James himself,
apparently, sees perfectly well) is so manifest
a mark. Hence, modified pragmatism must
either return to the much-abused correspondence theory or else accept most of the
absurd consequences to which radical pragmatism will lead us.   I see no way of avoiding
this dilemma. To stick to both interpretations and to use the word truth in " this large
loose way " is to contradict oneself. One cannot long ride upon two horses going in opposite directions ; one must choose between
them — or fall between them. Here as else-
where it will ultimately prove impossible to
run with the hare and hunt with the hounds.

We come now at last to a closer examination of the more radical pragmatic view
of the truth relation. And to understand
it thoroughly we must first notice a certain peculiarity in the use of the important
word *idea* which will go far to explain
the rather startling conclusion as to the

nature of truth to which it comes. When one first dips into the literature of pragmatism, one is somewhat mystified by recurrent phrases such as "the efficient working of an idea," "the idea's leading," etc. The various uses of this phrase point, I think, to an important difference in the intellectualistic and the pragmatic meaning of "idea" in connection with the truth problem. To the pragmatist the word idea means any representative content that leads to action or helps to bring order into a given situation. Hence Professor Dewey's synonym for it — namely, "plan of action." Thus the important thing about an idea to the pragmatist is, not its present relation to its object, but its influence upon conduct, its motive power or guiding force. Starting from the biological view of mind, the pragmatist insists that the purpose of thought is, not the acquisition of "truth," but the useful reaction of the organism upon the environment. Our "ideas" are thus essentially tools by which to handle and to

mold our experience. In short, they are
to the pragmatist, as I have said, not so
much beliefs or judgments as "plans of
action." From this it follows naturally and
almost inevitably that if the term *truth* is
to be applied to such "ideas," it cannot be
in the sense of "correspondence" as defined above.[1] As "a plan of action" is
not an assertion about something outside
our experience, but a way of grouping our
data or guiding our conduct, it cannot, of
course, be maintained that its "truth" depends
upon its relation to some outer reality.
One indeed may wonder that the word
truth should be applied to it at all, but once
so applied it is evident that there is nothing
for it to mean but usefulness and successful
action. A true idea in this sense is therefore one that works. This is especially
manifest in the case of the laws of science,
and I believe it was partly in this connection
that the pragmatic identification of truth with
usefulness first suggested itself. In so far as

[1] See p. 67

a scientific law is a mere short-hand expression for our experience, a mere formula for the condensed description of perceptions, its truth may be said to consist in its working.[1] In short, if an hypothesis proves itself a useful tool, it is forthwith called true, — true, that is, for immediate practical purposes, — and thus truth comes to be regarded as merely a "form of the good." As an example, Professor Dewey speaks of the invention of the telephone as a plan of action or idea that worked itself out, *i.e.* proved itself "true." And it is evident that if the word *true* is to be applied to inventions and similar plans of action at all, their "truth" is indeed "wholly an affair of making them true."

Before entering any criticism upon this view we must first note, for the sake of our own comprehension of the subject, the

[1] A deeper reflection, however, will inevitably raise the question *why* it works, and this can hardly be answered without reference to an environing reality; and thus we shall be brought back to the stricter sense of truth and the correspondence theory.

decidedly different meaning given to "idea" by the non-pragmatist. When the non-pragmatist says an "idea" is true, he uses the word to mean, not a plan of action, but a *judgment*. To him an idea which is not a judgment but is a mere image or plan or formula may lead in what direction it likes, it may be useful, successful, satisfactory, or their opposites, it may have any function you will, but it is not in the category of things that can be either true or false. In Bosanquet's words, "truth and falsehood are coextensive with judgment." [1] This being the case, the non-pragmatist does not and cannot consider "true" a predicate of the same kind as "benevolent" or "luminous" or "good" (as the pragmatist suggests), nor can he identify "truth" (in the sense of *trueness*) with a "function" or "leading" or "process."

And now to return to the pragmatist use of the word. Granted that, if the term *truth* is to be applied to a plan

[1] "Logic," Vol. 1, p. 72.

or purpose at all, it may as well mean successful execution as anything else, is not the use of the word in this connection, to say the least, unnatural and unnecessarily confusing? An invention may be useful and may work and be successful, my plan to go downtown may be wise and good, but to call either of them *true* would seem to be a step toward the invention of a new language.

And in spite of the undoubted truth in the biological view of mind, in spite of the fact that all ideas in some sense work themselves out, it is not true that all "ideas," judgments included, are merely plans of action. A judgment has at least two different aspects. From one point of view it is indeed a motor idea which influences conduct and works itself out. From another point of view it is an assertion about some reality not itself, and between it and that reality there is a relation which simply is not to be identified with the results of the judgment. This distinction between the two

I

aspects of a judgment, or between judgments and plans of action, seems to be quite overlooked by thinkers of widely different schools — *e.g.* by Professor Dewey, on the one hand, and Professor Royce,[1] on the other. These writers often deal with the subject of truth as if there were no distinction between judgment and purpose. Thus Professor Dewey tries to interpret judgments as plans of action by saying "the agreement, correspondence, is between purpose, plan, and its own execution, fulfillment."[2] But take any ordinary judgment such as "The sun is shining," or "The Greeks defeated the Persians

[1] Professor Moore has conclusively shown that if "idea" be taken to mean purpose, as Royce insists it shall, then the "truth" of an idea must be the fulfillment of the purpose within our experience, and not (as Royce says) the "correspondence between our ideas and their objects." To reach any relation between an idea and a reality outside of one's private stream of consciousness, Royce has practically to give up the purposive function of ideas as their most essential characteristic, and to speak of them as *representative*. See "The World and the Individual," Lectures I, VII, and VIII, and Moore's "Some Logical Aspects of Purpose," in "Studies in Logical Theory," pp. 341–382.

[2] "The Control of Ideas by Facts," *Jour. of Phil.*, Vol. IV, p. 202.

at Salamis." Where, in this case, is the plan and where the fulfillment? Or take at random any judgment from Professor Dewey's writings — for example, this, " Reality as such is an entire situation." How can this, at least without much forced and unnatural interpretation, be called "*a plan of action*"? To reduce all judgments to plans of action, to add that plans of action are true because they work, and to conclude that therefore the truth of a judgment consists in its working is hardly a cogent syllogism.

We come now to our final evaluation of the radical pragmatic view of the truth relation. For the radical pragmatist, truth is to be identified with "the psychological or biological processes by which it is pursued and attained."[1] " The effective working of the idea and its truth are one and the same thing," for it is "an experienced relation." The truth of an idea is "an event, a process, the process, namely, of its verifying itself, its verification."

[1] Professor Montague in the *Jour. of Phil.*, Vol. IV, p. 100.

One here feels tempted to ask: If truth be really identical with its proof, if it be nothing but the process of its verification, or the processes by which it is pursued and attained, what is it that is proved and verified, what is it that is pursued and attained? Are we verifying verification and pursuing pursuit? This indeed sounds like logomachy, but it really is not. For surely verification is verification of something. If you say it is the verification of the *idea*, just what do you mean? Certainly not the verification of the idea as a mere psychical existent. It must be, if it is anything at all, the verification of the idea's trueness, the demonstration that its claim is a rightful claim — *is* a rightful claim, mind you, not *will be* rightful. Here, let us say, is an assertion. As yet it is a mere claim. But it claims to be *true* — *i.e.* it claims that it *is* true. Now you verify it. It thereby becomes "a truth," but what you have verified is *that it was true already*. The very fact, therefore, that you verify presupposes that the trueness of the assertion or claim is something prior to and independent of its verification. The very use of the words *verification* and *proof* presupposes that truth is something distinct from any process of proof. Thus, though pragmatism may properly speak of successful and satisfactory experiences, it is hard to see how it can consistently use the term *verification* at all. To me, at least, it would seem as easy to lift oneself by one's boot straps as to comprehend how truth can consist in the process of its own verification, or how it (or anything else, for that matter) can *be* "the processes by which it is pursued and attained."

And now, to make matters perfectly clear, let us apply to this radical pragmatic meaning of truth the same illustration which was used in the preceding lecture to bring out the exact meaning of the correspondence theory. Poor Peter, you will remember, has a toothache, and John, who is thinking about his friend, has an idea that Peter has a toothache. As for the pragmatist the truth of an idea means its "efficient working," its "satisfactoriness," "the process of its verification," the truth of John's idea will "consist in" its satisfactoriness to John, in its efficient working, in its verifying itself. If it works, if it harmonizes with John's later experiences of Peter's actions, if it leads in a direction that is worth while, it is true (a statement to which, indeed, all might assent), and its truth *consists in* this working, this harmony, this verification process. John's thought, the pragmatist insists, *becomes* true only when it has worked out successfully, only when his later experience confirms it by being consistent with it, — for remember, truth is not verifiability, but the process of verification. "Truth happens to an idea. *It becomes* true, is *made* true by events." At the time when John had the thought about Peter the thought was *neither true nor false*, for the process of verification had not yet begun, nothing had as yet happened to the idea. To be sure, Peter had a toothache, just as John thought, but, all the same, John's thought was not true. It did not become true until several hours afterward, — in fact, we may suppose, not until Peter, having cured his toothache, told John about it. The thought, " Peter has a toothache, " thus, as it happens, turns out not to have been true while Peter actually had the toothache, and to have become true only after he had ceased to have a toothache. It became true only by being proved true, and its truth consisted in the process of its proof. One might, perhaps, be tempted to ask what it was that was proved, and to say to the pragmatist, Either the satisfactoriness, the successful leading, is a proof of something outside of John's immediate experience, something by which his idea is to be judged and justified (in which case truth ceases to be a mere verification process and becomes at least verifiability); or else it is merely John's subjective feeling of satisfaction and of successful leading and consistency, with no reference to anything else to justify it, — in which case it may indeed be pleasant and " good, " but it is hard to see why it should be called *true*. For suppose that at the same time with John's thought, Tom thinks Peter has *not* a toothache. Suppose that, being a little stupid and perhaps a little hard of hearing, he misinterprets John's actions and expressions, and that later on he is assured by some one equally misinformed that Peter certainly had no toothache. His thought thus works out, is successful, harmonizes with his later experience, is to him genuinely verified. The whole matter ends here, and he drops the question completely, never investigating further. Were the thoughts of both John and Tom true?

Now it will not do to respond, " No; Tom's thought was *not genuinely* verified. Only that thought was really verified and therefore true which *would have* worked out had both been investigated sufficiently." For what do you mean by " *sufficiently* "? Sufficiently for what? To argue thus would be to presuppose a criterion (apart from the leading of the thought) to which the thought must correspond if it is to be true. If you distinguish between a "genuine" verification and one that is only subjectively satisfactory, you appeal to some other criterion than the process of verification — in other words, you go over to the non-pragmatist's point of view. If, on the other hand, you stick to your pragmatic criterion and say that the truth of the thought consists in its *actual* satisfactoriness, then the question becomes pertinent: Were the thoughts of both boys true? Obviously they were, for both worked, both were satisfactory, both were verified. Hence it was true at the same time and in the same sense that Peter had a toothache and that Peter had not a toothache. Nor is there anything surprising in this, if truth be nothing but a particular kind of satisfactory experience. The principle of contradiction has no meaning and can no longer hold if truth be altogether within one's experience.

To set the problem in another light, let me put the following dilemma: Either there is a real and relevant world outside of your private stream of consciousness, — it may be a material world or one made up of other selves, — or else there is no such world and you need reckon only with your own private experiences. If you admit that this outer world exists and that you judge about the things or persons in it, you must also admit that the relation between these things or persons and your judgments of them is a fact which deserves to be recognized, and that, in one sense at least, the validity of your judgments depends on this relation. You may call this relation truth or reserve the term *truth* for something else, as you like; but, aside from terminology, once you recognize this relation and its bearing upon your judgments, you have essentially accepted the non-pragmatist's position. On the other hand, deny the existence of this relation and its relevancy to your judgments, and you either deny that there is any world outside your own conscious experience, or else you affirm that if such a world there be, it is nothing and never can be anything to you. And when you have done this, how far are you from solipsism? The non-pragmatist might be willing to admit that if this be a solipsistic world, "truth" might as well mean "effective working" as anything else.[1] But if it be a world in which one makes genuine references to outer realities that never come within one's private stream of consciousness, then the relation between those realities and one's judgment about them (a relation which from the nature of the case one can never experience) is something which cannot be neglected, but must be reckoned with, call it what you will.[2]

[1] It is interesting to note in this connection that all Professor Dewey's and Professor Moore's contributions to "Studies in Logical Theory," as well as most of Professor Dewey's more recent papers on truth and knowledge, could perfectly well have been written from the standpoint of solipsism — and, in fact, it is difficult to see how some of them could have been written from any other.

[2] The dilemma just proposed I suggested some time ago in the *Jour. of Phil.* (Vol. V, p. 131), and shortly afterward Professor Dewey replied to it in the course of an article of his in the same Journal (Vol. V, pp. 375–381). The gist of his reply is the insistence that my dilemma holds only for those who start with the "metaphysical" presupposition of a "mind," on one side, and "objects," on the other side, external

Before closing this lecture there is one
question which I should like to put to the

to it.   The pragmatist makes no such presupposition, but is
dealing with the problem only from the "logical standpoint,
to which the solipsistic controversy is irrelevant; — since a
logical inquiry is concerned only with inferential relations
among things, not with preconceptions about a lonely consciousness, or soul, or self."

Professor Dewey then goes on to put the following questions, which he considers the truly relevant ones in a logical
discussion (and which of course are expressed in such a way
as to indicate the pragmatist's answers) : "(1) Do ideas present themselves except in situations which are doubtful and
inquired into? . . . (2) Are the 'ideas' anything else except
the suggestions, conjectures, hypotheses, theories tentatively
entertained during a suspended conclusion? (3) . . . Do
they serve to direct observation, colligate data, and guide
experimentation, or are they otiose?   (4) If the ideas have
a function in directing the reflective process, does success in
performing the function have anything to do with the logical
worth or validity of the ideas?   (5) And finally, does this
matter of validity have anything to do with the question of
truth?   Does 'truth' mean something inherently different
from the fact that the conclusion of one judgment is itself
applicable in further situations of doubt and inquiry?"
(pp. 378-379.)

To these questions I think the following answers may be
made: (1) The first question is largely one of terminology.
For the sake of the argument let us grant that "ideas" are to
be found only in situations that are doubtful.   This is
certainly true of "ideas" in the sense Professor Dewey
attributes to the word.   I cannot see that this makes outer

pragmatist, — a definite answer to which might clear up some of the obscurities of

reference and correspondence any less essential to their meaning. (2) The second question is much more important. And here too let us accept the pragmatist's answer. "Ideas," let us say, are nothing but "suggestions," "conjectures," "hypotheses," "theories." But the question now arises, *What are* "suggestions," "theories," and the like? Are not conjectures, hypotheses, and theories *about* something? Do they not *mean* and *refer to* something not themselves, and is not this object of theirs often a contemporaneously existing thing? Is not a theory (when seriously maintained) a judgment that something *is* thus-and-so? And if this be the case, is not correspondence (in the sense I have defined) essential? If correspondence be ruled out, is not the whole content and significance of hypotheses and theories and the rest completely lost? And does not Professor Dewey grant substantially the whole non-pragmatist contention for correspondence when he writes, " The logical idea is short for a certain *judgment* about a thing. It states the way an object is *judged to be*, the way we *take it* in the inference process, as distinct from the way it actually may be." (p. 378.) (3) Certainly hypotheses and theories " serve to direct observation, guide experimentation," etc. But the prior and more important logical question (which Professor Dewey omits) is this : How do they do it? How comes it that they manage to succeed, that they lead us in the right direction, while certain other hypotheses fail? Theories, conjectures, etc., *of course* are instruments — who denies it? But the fundamental question is how it is possible for them to be instruments and what it is that makes some successful guides and some unsuccessful. So far as I can see the pragmatist has no answer to this. The non-

the subject, namely this : Is pragmatism true, and if so in what sense is it true?

And, first of all, is it true in the pragmatic sense? This is certainly a question which is very hard to answer. Since pragmatism has worked satisfactorily to the pragmatist, it evidently is true — to him. But with equal certainty it is not true to the non-

pragmatist answer of course is that hypotheses succeed in guiding experimentation in so far as they correspond to the already existing reality which is their object and which they *mean*. And this brings us to the fourth and fifth questions, to which the non-pragmatist answer is, in short, that the idea's success in performing its function is, no doubt, closely related to its validity and truth, but that the pragmatist has put the matter just the wrong way about, since it is the truth of the idea that makes it successful, not its success that makes it true. Its success is, if you like, the cause of *our recognition* of its truth, but the idea would never have succeeded at all had it not first been true.

The problem under discussion is indeed a logical one. But for that very reason it must deal with something more than "relations among things." It must consider also the meaning of those things. It must go deeper than the mere tracing out of what ideas *do*, as instruments, etc., in our experience. The previous question for logic is what these hypotheses are and mean, and how they act. And I still believe it impossible to face these questions squarely without accepting the one or the other horn of the dilemma proposed above.

pragmatist, for to him it is not satisfactory — it has not been verified. It is in exactly the position of any other unverified claim, and I hope we need not remind the pragmatist of his oft-repeated assertion that an unverified claim is not yet true. Pragmatism therefore (like so many other things in the pragmatic world) is both true and false at the same time. "And the best of the joke is," as Plato would say, that inasmuch as the non-pragmatists (as yet at least) far outnumber the pragmatists, it follows that pragmatism is true in only a small minority of cases. Of course no one (not even a humanist) would seriously start out to determine the truth of a doctrine by counting human heads; and yet if it really be the case that a doctrine is not true till verified, and is made true by verification, it would seem not altogether irrelevant to consider the number of those who regard its verification complete.

But it is evident that even if pragmatism were true in the pragmatic sense, this would

not satisfy the pragmatists. They believe
it is true in the non-pragmatic sense. Like
other rational beings, they are not satisfied
(except at times) with having their doctrine
accepted : they want to show that it *ought
to be* accepted. They believe it is true no
matter what people think, *already* true
whether verified or not. That is why they
are so eager to verify it. That is the very
presupposition of all their argument. They
insist, in other words, that the pragmatist
doctrine of truth is true in the non-pragmatic sense — true on the correspondence
theory of truth.

But alas! When they do that, they surrender the whole matter. To insist that a
doctrine must be verified in order to be true
and to add that this doctrine is true whether
verified or not, is as simple a manner as can
be found of contradicting oneself. Pragmatists, I am sure, will call this "logic-chopping "
— a simple and useful device when one has
been reduced to unavoidable self-contradiction. But inasmuch as this is altogether

a matter of logic I fail to see the force of the reproach. Inconsistency is the one great sin in thinking, and the inconsistency just pointed out runs through all the arguments by which the pragmatist seeks to prove his position. At every point he is — no doubt, unconsciously — making use of the very conception of truth which he is trying to refute; he is claiming for his doctrine the very kind of truth which he says is no truth at all. Consistently he should do the one or the other of two things: either give up his doctrine of truth; or else cease claiming that it is true and that logically we ought to accept it, and be content with enjoying it and proclaiming its satisfactoriness.

This latter is in fact the course which two of the leading pragmatists, in moments of insight, have actually taken. Speaking of the pragmatists and their universe of discourse, Professor James says, "Whether what they themselves say about that universe is objectively true, *i.e.* whether the pragmatic theory of truth is true *really*, they

K

cannot warrant, — they can only believe it."[1]
And in a spirit of candor, to illustrate further the fact that pragmatism is a mental
attitude rather than a logical position, he
compares it to general skepticism. This, he
says, "you can no more kill off by logic than
you can kill off obstinacy or practical joking.
This is why it is so irritating. . . . No more
can logic kill the pragmatist's behavior."
And I may say in passing that the history
of pragmatism amply confirms this assertion.

With equal consistency Dr. Schiller admits that "the pragmatic theory has to be
adopted before it can be verified," and that
therefore it would be absurd in pragmatism
to attempt to prove itself true to one who
had not first adopted it.[2]   It seems therefore
to be a case of *credo ut intelligam*.   One must
not expect to be convinced of the pragmatic
truth by vain arguments; one must taste and

---

[1] " The Pragmatist's Account of Truth," *Phil. Rev.*, Vol.
XVII, p. 16, note 2.

[2] See the instructive discussion between him and Professor Russell on this subject, in the *Jour. of Phil.*, Vol. IV,
pp. 235–243 and 482–494.

see that it is good. Nor are you to think this is mere idle jesting; it is the logical and inevitable outcome of the pragmatic doctrine of truth. When this is fully realized pragmatism may indeed still flourish — just as "practical joking" and "obstinacy" and "general skepticism" and unreasoning faith still flourish; but the consistent pragmatist at least will then cease to argue and begin rather to exhort; and pragmatism will be recognized as being primarily, not a serious philosophical doctrine, but rather one of the varieties of religious experience.

As I said at the beginning of this lecture, the pragmatic doctrine of truth is the key-stone to the whole edifice. And the inherent weakness in it which I have tried to point out affects fatally the entire superstructure. How it reappears in the pragmatic doctrine of knowledge I shall try to show in the following lecture.

LECTURE IV

PRAGMATISM AND KNOWLEDGE

LECTURE IV

PRAGMATISM AND KNOWLEDGE

EVERY one who has read with attention
the Fourth Book of Locke's famous Essay,
and has learned that knowledge is "nothing but the perception of the connection
and agreement or disagreement and repug-
nancy of any of our ideas," must have
noted with surprise the fact that one of
the four kinds of *agreement between our
ideas* is what Locke calls "real existence."
"The fourth and last sort" (of agreement), says he, "is that of actual and real
existence agreeing to any idea "— that is,
the agreement of something which "has
a real existence outside the mind," such as
"God," with our idea of it. It is hard, of
course, to see what "ideas" agree in this
fourth kind of knowledge, or how the agreement of an idea with something outside the

mind can be classed under knowledge at all if knowledge be "nothing but the perception of the agreement of our ideas." This inconsistency in Locke's theory of knowledge has often been pointed out and indeed is perfectly clear. But what concerns us here is the fact that it seems to be hereditary and has been handed down, like the original sin of Adam or — what is worse — like an "innate idea," to Locke's lineal descendants, our friends the pragmatists. To make this clear, however, will require an entire lecture; and we shall therefore devote this hour to a consideration of the pragmatic view of knowledge.

In considering pragmatism's doctrine of truth, you will remember, we found it helpful to outline first of all the non-pragmatist's view, for by noting what the pragmatist denied we were better able to understand what he affirmed. The same method will be of even more value here; hence before trying to get at the pragmatic meaning of knowledge I shall take up the view which pragmatism attacks. This view has had many formulations, but the one first suggested, by the great "intellectualist," Plato, is perhaps as satisfactory as any. It is found in the Theætetus and is in these words: Knowledge is "true opinion accompanied with reason." There is more substance in this very brief definition than may appear on the surface, and to make its meaning clear it should be divided, like a preacher's text, into firstly, secondly, and thirdly. Firstly, then, knowledge is a certain kind of *opinion*, *i.e.* it is a *judgment* or *thought about* something. Secondly, it must be true. And, thirdly, the individual who holds it true must have sufficient reason for so doing — he must be able to prove it true, at least to himself. A word of further explanation about each of these may not be out of place.

Perhaps the most important, because the most fundamental, of these three points is the first. Opinion is *about* something, it means or points to something not itself, and hence involves "transcendence." This of course is a terrifying term, and the prag-matist (who denies transcendence) makes capital out of its terrors. Really, however, there is nothing dreadful about this word, — it is a very simple thing after all, — though no doubt sufficiently mysterious to those who start out with the presupposi-tion that it is impossible. It means simply this: that when we "know" or "mean" something, the object of our thought is not our thought itself and may even be some-thing completely outside of our experience, past, present, or future. If any of you are unfamiliar with the term and still think it something very hard and "metaphysical," and that it is too "abstract" to be accepted by common sense, let me put you this ques-tion and ask your answer: When you are thinking of your neighbor's headache, do you mean by that headache something in *your* experience, or something out of your experience but in his? If you mean the latter, you are a believer in transcendence. This belief, in fact, is very much older than " Philosophy " and is one of the fundamental principles of common sense — as Professor James himself would doubtless tell you. It is, in short, simply the belief that you can *mean* something which is entirely outside of your own experience.

To be sure, if we take the view that every content of consciousness, our knowing thought included, is merely so much psychic stuff and nothing else, that it is simply *felt*, like an abdominal pain, and has no reference to anything outside itself, then, of course, transcendence becomes a mystery, because, in fact, meaning itself becomes a mystery. And so the pragmatist asks, *How can* a psychic state transcend itself? *How can* it mean anything but itself?—One might respond by the question, *How can* time pass? *How can* a thing move?— There may be many answers to questions such as these; but the simplest and certainly the most empirical is just this : that as a fact things *do* move, time *does* pass, and our thoughts *do mean* things other than themselves. Transcendence is merely one of those ultimately simple things which, just because they are ultimate and simple elements of experience, can never be explained further, nor analyzed further, but must be merely recognized and accepted. That it is in one sense a mystery is of course perfectly obvious : so is consciousness. But to prove by this that it is impossible, and to mystify ourselves over it, is simply gratuitous mystification. The truth is, a cognitive idea — a thought which *means* its object — has another characteristic than merely that of being felt — like a mosquito bite. It has that too, of course ; it is a genuine part of the stream of experience. But it is more than that. It *means* something besides itself and, it may be, something outside of the entire stream of consciousness to which it belongs. And to shut our eyes to this peculiarity of our thought in the interests of simplification and "concreteness" is very unempirical, and as poor psychology as it is epistemology.

So much for what is meant by saying that knowledge is opinion. And now the *secondly* and *thirdly* of our text from Plato may be easily disposed of. The secondly, in fact, — namely that the opinion must be true, — has already been explained in my two lectures on truth. But to be in possession of genuine knowledge we must have something more than opinion which happens to be true; we must, according to the traditional philosophy, be also in possession of reasons which *prove* the opinion to be true. This is a subordinate point so far as our present purposes are concerned and may be shortly dismissed. In brief, it may be said that whatever sort of proof any one — pragmatist or non-pragmatist — believes in, and has to furnish, is here relevant. Of course I cannot get outside my own experience and compare my idea with the outer reality — your headache, let us say — which it means.

This kind of proof is out of the question, and quite as much so for pragmatists as for others, as Professor James admits.[1] But there are other ways of proving — notably the negative method of consistency, and the scientific (or pragmatic) method of noting results. Only the former method, to be sure, gives absolute demonstration, and the latter alone, even at its best, will not enable us to prove the truth of our ideas any more completely and absolutely than science can prove that the sun will rise to-morrow, or than history can prove that it rose yesterday, or than pragmatism can refute solipsism (a performance which is particularly difficult for pragmatism). We can seldom attain the absolute kind of proof furnished by mathematics. But so purely theoretical an ideal of demonstration belongs rightly to an effete rationalism, and the pragmatist is certainly

[1] Pragmatists "cannot do without the wider knower [who should compare ideas with objects] any more than they can do without the reality, if they want to *prove* a case of knowing. . . . Whether what they themselves say about the whole universe is objectively true they cannot warrant — they can only believe it." — *Phil. Rev.*, Vol. XVII, p. 16, note 2.

the last man who should demand its realization. In short, the transcendence-view of knowledge is no more inconsistent with proof than is any other. And with this enough has been said for our present purposes of exegesis, and I trust the text from Plato is now sufficiently clear.

I have gone thus into detail with the ordinary view of knowledge because it is this view which pragmatism denies. Our next aim must therefore be to get a clear notion of the theory of knowledge set up by the pragmatists as a substitute for the one rejected. The essential characteristic of this pragmatic view is the attempt to avoid transcendence (in the sense outlined above), and to present knowledge as a concrete experience process entirely within the conscious life of the individual.

To be more explicit, knowledge is, in the words of Professor Dewey, "a doubt-inquiry-answer experience." It arises when our reality, our facts, are somehow unsatisfactory and self-discrepant, and it has a definite, practical function, namely the reorganization of our experience upon the basis of a plan of action, which brings definite good results and makes our experience harmonious and satisfactory once more. Mere immediate experience is not knowledge; to be knowledge it must be in some ways disharmonious or insufficient, it must point to or suggest some sort of experience not itself. This further experience when it comes must bring harmony into consciousness once more, which by fulfilling the need of the preceding experience shall abolish knowledge by substituting immediacy. There are thus three stages in the knowing process. The first is that of "doubt" in which the facts of experience show themselves self-discrepant, disharmonious, and in need of rearrangement or supplementation. In the second stage — or that of "inquiry" — an "idea" or "plan or action" or tentative arrangement of present and absent facts is suggested and tried. Finally, in the third stage this "plan" is found to work, and experience once more becomes harmonious and is no longer cognitional.

To illustrate by two examples of Professor Dewey's: I hear a fearsome noise and am frightened. I do not understand it. My situation is self-discrepant. Therefore I set out to solve the enigma. I make the hypothesis that the cause of the noise is the window curtain rattling in the wind. This leads me to certain actions which result in the verification of my hypothesis. My experience now is one of satisfaction rather than of knowledge, but I am able to look back at the second stage, where I formed the hypothesis, and see that it was cognitional. Or, I smell a sweet odor. I wonder what it is. The odor thus ceases to be *merely* an odor and becomes transformed into a cognitional odor which *means* a rose. This leads me to certain acts which result in the full realization of the rose by all my senses. In short, to sum up: "An experience is a knowledge if in its quale there is an experienced distinction and connection of two elements of the following sort: one means or intends the presence of the other

L

in the same fashion in which itself is already present, while the other is that which, while not present in the same fashion, must become so present if the meaning or intention of its companion or yoke fellow is to be fulfilled through an operation it sets up." [1]

Professor James's view of knowledge, though varying in some details from that of Professor Dewey, is not essentially different. Especially in the attempt to avoid transcendence and to make knowledge a thoroughly "concrete" process that "lives inside the tissue of experience," are the two views at one. To use a distinction of Professor James's, knowledge is not "*saltatory*" but "*ambulatory*" — it is not a leap from idea to object over an empty chasm, but an experienced process of gradual transition every step of which is felt. "Intervening experiences are as indispensable foundations for a concrete relation of cognition as intervening space is for a relation of distance.

[1] Professor Dewey, "The Experimental Theory of Knowledge," *Mind*, Vol. XV, p. 301.

Cognition, whenever we take it concretely, means determinate ambulation, through intermediaries, from a *terminus a quo* to or toward a *terminus ad quem*. As the intermediaries are other than the termini and connected with them with the usual associative bonds, there would appear to be nothing especially unique about the process of knowing. They fall wholly within experience; and we need use, in describing them, no other categories than those which we employ in describing other natural processes." [1]

In describing Professor James's view of knowledge I can probably do no better than continue to quote from his own lucid exposition. " Suppose me to be sitting here in my library in Cambridge, at ten minutes walk from ' Memorial Hall,' and to be thinking truly of the latter object. My mind may have before it only the name, or it may have a clear image, or it may

[1] " A Word more about Truth," *Jour. of Phil.*, Vol. IV, p. 399.

have a very dim image of the hall, but such intrinsic differences in the image make no difference in its cognitive function. Certain *extrinsic* phenomena, special experiences of conjunction, are what impart to the image its knowing office. . . . If I can lead you to the hall, and tell you of its history and present uses; if in its presence I now feel my idea to be *continued ;* if the associates of the image and of the felt hall run parallel, so that each term of the one context corresponds serially, as I walk, with an answering term of the other; why then my soul was prophetic, and my idea must be, and by common consent would be, called cognizant of reality. That percept was what it *meant*, for into it my idea has passed by conjunctive experiences of sameness and fulfilled intention. Nowhere is there jar, but every later moment matches and corroborates an earlier.

" In this matching and corroborating, taken in no transcendental sense, but denoting definitely felt transitions, lies all

that the knowing of a percept by an idea
can possibly contain or signify.   Wherever
such transitions are felt, the first experience
knows the last one.   Knowledge thus lives
inside the tissue of experience.   It is *made;*
and made by relations that unroll themselves
in time.   Whenever certain intermediaries
are given, such that, as they develop toward
their terminus, there is experience from
point to point of one direction followed,
and finally of one process fulfilled, the result is that their starting point thereby becomes a knower and their terminus an
object meant or known.   That is all that
knowing (in the simple case considered) can
be known-as, that is the whole of its
nature put into experiential terms.   Whenever such is the sequence of our experiences,
we may freely say that we had the terminal
object ' in mind ' from the outset, although
at the outset nothing was there in us but a
flat piece of substantive experience like any
other, with no self-transcendency about it,
and no mystery save the mystery of coming

into existence and of being followed by other pieces of substantive experience, with conjunctively transitional experiences between." [1]

The prime characteristic of the pragmatic view of knowledge is, as I have said, its attempt to avoid transcendence. It is that which makes it unique and distinguishes it from other views. Before examining for ourselves, however, the possibility of knowledge without transcendence, I should point out that each of the leading pragmatists admits (at times at least) a kind of transcendence. In this, however, they do not seem to be entirely at one. Professor Dewey points to a transcendence within the individual's experience, while Professor James goes farther and admits a reference to things entirely outside of it.

In his admirably clear article, " The Experimental Theory of Knowledge," from which I have already quoted, Professor Dewey points out that a cognitional ex-

[1] "A World of Pure Experience," *Jour. of Phil.*, Vol. I, pp. 539-540.

perience "is contemporaneously aware of meaning something beyond itself." The odor which knows the rose, for instance, is not merely an odor, not merely "a flat piece of substantive experience like any other." If it were merely that, there would be no question of knowledge, according to Dewey. It must have the additional quality of meaning or intending "something beyond itself." "The odor knows the rose; the rose is known by the odor; and the import of each term is constituted by the relationship in which it stands to the other." Now in all this I, of course, agree. But I should like to point out that this *meaning* or *intending* of something beyond itself by the cognitional experience does not consist in and is not constituted by the subsequent concrete steps of fulfillment. The cognitional experience or idea *already* means or intends the rose before the fulfilling experiences come; and should consciousness suddenly cease or be turned into a new direction and the fulfilling experiences never come, it would still be true that the idea in question did really mean and intend the rose.

But if a cognitive experience may thus mean a fulfilling experience which has not yet come and which possibly may never come, why may it not equally well mean or intend an experience which by the nature of the case never can come? I recognize that Professor Dewey here admits only a reference from one part to another of the individual's experience; but if the possibility of such reference is thus once admitted, why may not the individual's thought refer to and mean something in some one else's experience? If it can mean or intend something beyond itself at all, it is hard to see why this something must be one kind of experience rather than another. And if you grant this, the whole non-pragmatist view of transcendence is admitted.

In some respects Professor James would go even farther in his concessions than Professor Dewey, for he frankly admits the reference of our thoughts to things quite without our own actual experience. " The known," he tells us, may be " a *possible* experience, either of that subject or of another, to which the said conjunctive transitions *would* lead if sufficiently prolonged."[1]   This, however, in Professor James's view, does not involve transcendence, apparently because experience in general is nowhere transcended, because there are connecting links of concrete experience actual or at least possible between my thought and its object; and also because, as he maintains, my thought's reference to its object consists just in those actual or possible "conjunctive transitional experiences."

For one, I confess it is hard for me to see how this avoids transcendence. The battle of Marathon, for instance, is certainly not a part of my experience, yet is known by me; and the fact that there are *possible* experiences between me and it and

[1] "A World of Pure Experience," *Jour. of Phil.*, Vol. I, p. 538.

that if I were now 2400 years old I might
have witnessed the battle, does not make
it any the less true that my actual experience — and apparently *all* actual experience
— has to be transcended if I am to know
or to mean it.   In fact, once it is admitted
that the idea's object may be within some
one else's experience, the whole transcendence controversy would seem to be settled,
and the non-pragmatist position granted.

But this Professor James would not admit.
Knowledge, he insists, is ambulatory, not
saltatory.   The meaning or reference of an
idea is not a leap to its object but a concrete and experienced process.   " Knowing
is *made* by the ambulation through the
intervening experiences." [1]   " If we believe,
with common sense, in so-called ' sensible '
realities, the idea may not only lead us
toward its object, but may put the latter into
our very hand, make it our immediate sensation.   But if, as most reflective people
opine, sensible realities are not true realities,

[1] *Jour. of Phil.*, Vol. IV, p. 399.

but only their appearances, our idea brings
us at least so far, puts us in touch with
reality's most authentic substitutes and
representatives."[1] They lead us as near to
the real object which we mean as we can
ever get; and there, of course, they stop.
The pity is that Professor James's explanation stops there too, and hence fails to
touch upon the most important part of the
problem — the relation, namely, between
these last terms within our experience and
the outer objects of which these experiences of ours are only "substitutes and
representatives." One feels like asking, Is
this relation ambulatory or saltatory? If it
be ambulatory, who is it that ambulates?
It is certainly not we, for we can get no
farther directly than to the "substitutes
and representatives," never to the "true
realities" which they mean. Or is it the
object that ambulates? If knowledge be an
experience process, who experiences it? And
if the relation between the "true realities"

and their "representatives" be a saltatory relation, is not knowledge saltatory, and are we not forced back to the non-pragmatist's view outlined at the beginning of this lecture?

The truth seems to be that genuine transcendence is unavoidable wherever the cognitive idea — the knowing thought — means to have for its object something besides itself. And if this object be something within another's life, then there must be a genuine transcendence of the individual's entire experience — a leap from idea to object with no felt transition — as, for example, when I think of *your* headache. There are no felt transitions between our experiences. My consciousness never runs into yours. Nor does it solve the difficulties of this particular problem to point out, as Professor James does,[1] that our minds have *space* in common; for they remain apart none the less, and there is no *experience of transition* between them. In Professor James's own words: "Neither

[1] *Jour. of Phil.*, Vol. I, pp. 565–568.

contemporaneity nor proximity in space, nor similarity of quality and content are able to fuse thoughts together which are sundered by this barrier of belonging to different personal minds. The breaches between such thoughts are the most absolute breaches in nature." [1]

In his "Psychology," Professor James has rightly laid great emphasis on the difference between a succession of experiences and an experience of succession. Now the pragmatist theory of knowledge requires both of these. It must have an unbroken succession of intermediating experiences, and it must also have, with this, the experience of the succession or transition. But in no case where my object is something in your experience can either of these essentials be proved to be present; and one of them is certainly absent. If there be a succession of intermediaries between my thought and your headache — or between my thought and Nebuchadnezzar's headache — neither you nor I

[1] "Psychology," p. 153.

nor Nebuchadnezzar ever experiences the
succession. *My experiences break off where
yours begin.* This fact is of great importance, for it bars out the sense of transition
and fulfillment which forms so important an
element in the pragmatist description of
knowledge, — the sense of fulfillment due to
a continuous passage from the original idea
to the known object. If this comes at all
when I know your headache, it comes not
with the object but quite on my side of the
"epistemological gulf." The gulf is still
there to be transcended.

But let us examine a case in which the
object and the thought which means it are
both within the same stream of experience —
the type of case best fitted to exemplify the
pragmatist view of knowledge and the easiest
for it to explain. And to make sure that
our example is orthodox, let us take the case
outlined by Professor James. Suppose,
then, I am sitting in Cambridge, at some
distance from Memorial Hall, and have
in my mind "nothing but a flat piece of

substantive experience with no self-transcendency about it." This flat piece of substantive experience is an image of Memorial Hall. It is followed by a series of transitional experiences, muscle and joint sensations, visual and auditory sensations, which change and succeed each other rapidly, and connected with them there is an experience of one direction being followed. Finally, one of these exfoliating experiences is the percept of Memorial Hall, and with this percept comes a sense of process fulfilled. This succession of experiences crowned by the sense of fulfillment, says the pragmatist, *is* knowledge. And now let me point out one peculiarity of this view. When the intermediaries have been experienced and the process is fulfilled — when, that is, we have got our percept of Memorial Hall — "the result is," as Professor James says, "that their starting point *thereby becomes* a knower and their terminus an object meant or known."[1] This, of course, is an exact statement of the necessary

[1] *Jour. of Phil.*, Vol. I, p. 540.

outcome of the doctrine. The italics are mine, but they might as well have been in the original. The idea of Memorial Hall, which we called the knowing thought, and which started the process going, does not become a "knower" till long after it has vanished and has been replaced by many intermediaries and finally by the fulfilling percept. In like manner, Memorial Hall was never "known" nor even "meant" till then. Hence the "*knower*" did not know nor mean anything so long as it existed, but became a knower only after it had ceased to exist altogether; and in like manner Memorial Hall was never *known* nor *meant* until the idea which knew and meant it had altogether vanished.

Where, then, one naturally asks, does knowledge come in? Not at the *terminus a quo*, for the idea has not yet become a knower — its knowing, according to the pragmatist, *consists in* the intermediaries and the fulfilling experience. Not at the *terminus ad quem*, for now there is no longer a knower but merely a direct experience. Not in the intermediaries, for with them we have neither knower nor fulfillment. Of course it may be said that when at last I see Memorial Hall, the original image of it returns, hence is present as a knower. But this will not fit the theory for several reasons. In the first place, as every psychologist knows, the original image cannot return ; one *like* it may come, but not the same identical experience. And indeed, if it be this reproduced idea, now present, that is the real knower, why speak of the original idea and the intermediaries at all? Why not simply describe your present experience?

Or, possibly, the pragmatist may say that when the fulfilling experience has come, we look back at the original idea and see that it — what? Knew the object? No, for it was not yet a knower. Was true? No, for truth consists in the intermediating and fulfilling experiences which at that time did not yet exist. Shall we say that it resembled or was like the percept of Memorial Hall?

M

But no, for it may have been very unlike,
and even if it were very like the percept, this
way of putting things would be a reversion
to the " copy theory " in its crudest and most
unpragmatic form.   Or shall we say simply
that it started the process going?   This undoubtedly would be true; but what of it?
Does it help us out at all in seeing where
knowledge comes in? The sensation of
hunger might have started me toward Memorial Hall quite as well; does the sensation of
hunger therefore "become a knower" when I
look at the Hall?   The truth is, when the
knowing thought which already means something not itself is replaced by "a flat piece of
substantive experience like any other," knowledge must at once vanish away, and we shall
have left merely a succession of experiences
such as the proverbial polyp might enjoy.
To have a succession of experiences (or even
an experience of succession) is one thing; to
know is quite another.

There is one more characteristic of the
pragmatist view of knowledge which should

be noted before we bring this lecture to a close; namely, its (perfectly consistent) refusal to insist that knowledge must be *true*. It does insist, of course, that knowledge must be true in the pragmatic sense of being satisfactory, etc.; but, quite properly, it fails to say anything about its being true in any other sense. This is as it should be; and yet it forces one to ask some such question as this: In knowledge do we really know?

Take, for example, Professor Dewey's illustration already used. I hear a fearsome noise and am filled with fright; then, looking back on my experience and analyzing it, I come to the conclusion that it was only the noise of the window curtain. And to vary the illustration a little at this point, let us suppose that you too have been frightened by the noise, but come to the conclusion that it was due to a fluttering awning. And let us add that you were right and that it *really was* the awning (if the pragmatist will allow us the use of such an expression), but that I never come to know this and that the window-curtain theory remains my final and (to me) perfectly satisfactory solution of the problem. Is this solution *knowledge?*   Do I *know* that the curtain was the cause of the noise?

Now if the pragmatist answers in the negative, and maintains that this is not a genuine case of knowledge, then it follows that knowledge is not merely a process in which a final opinion or "experience" is substituted for a former experience because more satisfactory to the experiencer. It is more than "an answering or telling experience in which an unquestioned thing replaces a dubious thing." It must not merely be an *answering* experience; it must give the *true answer* ("*true*" here being used in the non-pragmatist sense). And it cannot then be defined in terms of experience alone as a "doubt-inquiry-answer experience." The complete definition of knowledge must include something which distinguishes the true from the false, a reference to a reality beyond the experience itself which makes it true. It must be defined in terms not essentially different from those of Plato — "true opinion with reason."

But the pragmatist probably will take the other course and deny that correspondence to an outer reality is necessary. He will identify knowledge with the psychological process in the individual's experience leading to the final solution of the problem and the sense of satisfaction and fulfillment — the answering experience which substitutes the unquestioned thing for the dubious thing — in short, with the "window-curtain theory" of our illustration. He will say that if this is in all respects satisfactory to me, it is for me knowledge — quite aside from the question whether it is "true" or not. Or, rather, he will of course insist (if he be consistent) that my theory *is* true since it satisfies me and silences my doubt. It is true, that is, in the pragmatic sense.

I am not altogether certain, however, that the pragmatist will be willing to maintain this position permanently. For it clearly

has its difficulties, — difficulties which even
a pragmatist must eventually come to see.
If there were only one individual involved,
the difficulty might be glossed over; but
you will remember that, according to our example, there were two of us concerned, and
that while I "knew" the cause of the noise
was the curtain, you "knew" it was the awning. Each of us now goes his way fully
persuaded in his own mind. The final experience of each has all the ear marks which
Dewey and James describe as belonging to
the final term in the knowledge process.
For, be it observed, there is not one thing
in the pragmatist description of knowledge
which would not apply perfectly well to a
case of mistaken opinion in which the individual had and always retained a complete
sense of certainty. Here, in fact, is the crucial point of the controversy — the pragmatists insisting that knowledge can be
sufficiently described and defined without going beyond the experience of the knowing
individual; the non-pragmatists maintaining

that a reference to something outside of his experience is essential.   And, in a sense, the whole problem may be said to hinge on the question of mistaken or false opinion.   How will the pragmatist interpret this?— For surely he cannot deny that we are often mistaken even when we feel and continue to feel most sure. — The question really is unavoidable : When one is mistaken but satisfied, does he know?   Did you and I both *know* the cause of the fearsome noise when we had contrary opinions concerning it?

The pragmatist cannot respond that he means by knowledge only that opinion or " experience " which works out; for by hypothesis both opinions work out, both are satisfactory so far as investigated, so far as " worked."   And if he amends his statement so as to say that he means by knowledge only that opinion which *would* work if carried out, then he is unconsciously surrendering his whole case by smuggling in the idea of a conditioning environment which determines whether or not the " ex-

perience " *can* work, and which cannot itself
be identified with the experience or any part
of it.   He would be saying that after all it is
not the " satisfactoriness " of the experience
that makes it knowledge but rather the experience's *right to be satisfactory*, — a right
determined not by itself but by the nature
of the conditioning environment.   And so he
would be back with us again in the " mystery " of transcendence.

In short, it would seem that the pragmatist
is logically shut up to the one or the other
of two alternatives : either he must accept
transcendence in the old-fashioned sense, or
else he must maintain that there is no essential difference between true and false opinion
and that both are equally worthy of the name
knowledge, so long as each remains satisfactory to its possessor.   You cannot lift yourself by your boot straps ; nor give the length
of a river in terms of itself and with no objective unit; nor distinguish knowledge from
error by mere description of what happens
within one individual's experience.   Unless

there be transcendence, there is no criterion for judging between two opinions, except, of course, the relative subjective satisfactoriness of the two. And if contradictory opinions may both be knowledge, provided they are equally satisfactory to their possessors, then each man is the measure of all things with a vengeance, and it becomes the most blatant sort of self-contradiction for the pragmatist to try to prove *his* view to be *knowledge* and *ours error.* — As I have said in another connection, the thing for him to do is to *feel* — and to exhort.

There is an old story, which many of you may have heard, of a countryman going to a circus and standing spellbound and incredulous before a dromedary with its many humps and its impossible legs and neck. All the other sight-seers passed out of the menagerie, but he still remained with his eyes riveted on the beast. Finally, at the end of half an hour, he drew himself together, with the proud consciousness of the triumph of reason over the senses, and exclaimed: " Hell! There ain't any such animal!"

The attitude of our pragmatist friends toward transcendence is not essentially different from that of the farmer toward the dromedary. They cannot frame a judgment about anything outside of themselves, they cannot even claim the truth of their own theory, without presupposing the thing they deny. It is there, plainly, before their very eyes. Yet they bravely maintain their stand — like the farmer. And their reason for so doing, moreover, seems to be essentially the same as his. There couldn't be any such animal as a dromedary because it looked so different from the cow and the pig and the other beasts of the farm. So there can't be any such thing as transcendence because it is so different from the " concrete " experience processes studied by psychology. Hence what passes for transcendence must be explained away in terms of experience " with no mystery about it." To reduce all mental states to their simplest terms is certainly one of the proper aims of the student of psychology and epistemology, and, perhaps, it is not surprising that the pragmatist seeks to regard the cognitive idea which means its object as "nothing but a flat piece of substantive experience" with no nonsense about it.   To interpret the knowing thought as belonging to the same general class as the mosquito bite is doubtless a consummation devoutly to be wished.   But, unfortunately, the knowing thought resists any such simplification.   It *means* more than it *is*.   If transcendence is a mystery, it is at least a very real mystery, and the attempt to ignore it or to explain it away is bound to end in failure. It is not true that everything is like everything else.   There are several things in this world which are *sui generis*.   One of these things is the dromedary.   Another is knowledge.

LECTURE V

PRAGMATISM AND RELIGION

SOMEHOW or other pragmatism has got itself pretty generally associated in the public mind with religion. It seems to be the common impression that at this critical moment in the warfare of religion with agnosticism the pragmatists have come up to the help of the Lord against the mighty, and that, thanks to their new-forged and new-fashioned weapons, victory is secure. It is this belief, I suppose, which more than anything else explains the wide and growing popularity of the new philosophy. For, after all, no other philosophical problems have so great and so permanent a hold upon the interests of the people at large as have those that deal with religion. For this very reason, moreover, no philosophical ideas deserve and require more careful scrutiny than those which affect the religious views of the community. Since, therefore, there is so considerable a tendency to-day to throw one's cap in air and shout, "The sword of the Lord and of Pragmatism!" it behooves all those who have the interests of religion at heart to look carefully into the question whence pragmatism has gained its religious reputation and how well it deserves it. What is the nature and the temper of this newly patented pragmatic sword, and is it so sure a defense that we may with safety throw aside for it our older weapons? Just what is it that pragmatism proves and how does it prove it? If we trust our religious beliefs to its defense, just what surety have we that they will be defended and that when we get them back again they will still be recognizable? When the question is put in this way, the controversy over the meaning and validity of pragmatism ceases to be a merely academic matter, and is seen to be fraught with truly human and living interest.

Now in itself pragmatism is neither religious nor irreligious. It is essentially a doctrine or group of kindred doctrines concerning the nature of meaning, truth, and knowledge. It is epistemological and logical rather than metaphysical, theological, ethical, or religious. Hence in completing our discussion of knowledge, truth, and meaning, I have finished all that I shall have to say of the fundamental principles of pragmatism. If not over-scrupulous about consistency, it is possible to hold any one of several different views on metaphysics, religion, ethics, etc., and still be a pragmatist,—and in fact on many important metaphysical questions our leading pragmatists hold very divergent positions. While all this is true, however, it must not be overlooked that one's epistemology is pretty sure to color or even determine one's metaphysics, and therefore to influence one's religious views — so far as these are a matter of reasoning at all. Whence two things follow. In the first place, there is a certain family resemblance between the metaphysical and religious

N

views of most pragmatists, due not so much to logic as to disposition; to minds that hold the pragmatic view of truth the same general type of philosophic attitude seems to be natural. And secondly, the fundamental principles of pragmatic epistemology when consistently applied to certain philosophical and theological problems ought to determine, and logically must determine, one's attitude toward them, whether as a matter of fact they *do* determine the attitude of individual pragmatists or not.

It will, in fact, be recalled that at the beginning of these lectures I set down as one of the characteristic features of pragmatism its attempt to work out a theory of reality. Unfortunately for our purposes, however, this is as yet only an attempt; the pragmatic view of reality is as yet in so embryonic and unformed a condition that it would be premature and unfair for a non-pragmatist to try to state it. Its central doctrine seems to be that reality is not stiff and static and independent of us, but is *made* largely by our interests and desires; and that "knowledge *is* reality making a particular and specified sort of change in itself."[1] Just how far pragmatism will carry this general doctrine and just what it will make out of it remains as yet to be seen. It is to be hoped, in particular, that Professor Dewey will elaborate his view of reality and formulate it in terms which the non-pragmatist reader can understand. In its present incipient state, as I have said, it would be unfair for one who is not a pragmatist and cannot speak with any authority to attempt to expound it, and much more unfair for him to criticise it. I shall, therefore, leave the subject here, and simply refer any of you who would like to know more about it to the following sources: Schiller's essay on "The Ethical Basis of Metaphysics" in "Humanism,"[2] and his two essays entitled "The Making of Truth" and "The Making

[1] Professor Dewey, "Does Reality possess Practical Character?" in the volume of "Essays Philosophical and Psychological, in Honor of William James," p. 59.

[2] pp. 1–17.

of Reality," respectively, in his "Studies in Humanism";[1] Dewey's contributions to the "Studies in Logical Theory,"[2] his series of papers on "The Control of Ideas by Facts" in Volume IV of the *Journal of Philosophy*,[3] and his most recent statement on the subject (already quoted from) in the Columbia *Festschrift* for James; namely, "Does Reality possess Practical Character?";[4] and James's lecture on "Pragmatism and Humanism" in his "Pragmatism."[5]

But while I shall not venture to expound the pragmatic view of reality in general, I believe I shall be justified in discussing the attitude of pragmatism toward the particular kind of metaphysical problem referred to in the title of this lecture — the religious problem. On this many of the leading pragmatists have very decided views, — views determined, as I said above, largely by natural disposition, — and these views they have expressed clearly and at considerable length.

[1] pp. 179–203, 421–451. [2] pp. 1–85.
[3] pp. 197–203, 253–259, 309–319.
[4] pp. 53–80. [5] pp. 239–270.

Moreover, the fundamental epistemological principles of pragmatism have a necessary and direct bearing upon the religious problems which even a non-pragmatist has a right to point out. The present lecture, therefore, falls naturally into two parts, — it must deal with the general attitude which most pragmatists by temperament hold toward religion, and, secondly, it must outline more definitely and in particular the view which pragmatism as such *ought* to hold if its presuppositions are to be logically carried out.

The same temperamental bias which makes the pragmatist lean toward a voluntaristic psychology and define truth in terms of value usually tends to make him also a pluralist rather than a monist, a believer in free will rather than in determinism, an upholder of the strenuous, dynamic, dramatic view of the universe in which there are real dangers and genuine crises, rather than an advocate of absolutism with its peaceful and static world in which everything is saved from all eternity. To the pragmatist of the James-Schiller type, religion means something very vital and real. The religious view of the world for him is not just the naturalistic view under a new light and with a new name, as is the case too often with some Hegelian philosophers; it is a genuinely and practically different world — different in the pragmatic sense of *making a difference*. " Religion," says Professor James, " in her fullest exercise of function, is not a mere illumination of facts already elsewhere given, not a mere passion, like love, which views things in a rosier light. It is indeed that, but it is something more ; namely, a postulator of new *facts* as well. The world interpreted religiously is not the materialistic world over again, with an altered expression; it must have, over and above the altered expression, *a natural constitution* different at some points from that which a materialistic world would have. It must be such that different events can be expected in it, different conduct be required." [1]

[1] " The Varieties of Religious Experience," p. 518.

And, to be more explicit, the pragmatic temper finds especially congenial the psychological rather than the scholastic view of religion. It likes to look upon religion neither as a divine revelation nor as a philosophical construction, but as an essentially human product and one which gets its justification and authority, and its proof (so far as it has any), from the very nature of man, and from its own usefulness to man. Professor James speaks of his method of evaluating religions as "the elimination of the humanly unfit and the survival of the humanly fittest, applied to religious beliefs"; and, he adds, "if we look at history candidly and without prejudice, we have to admit that no religion has ever in the long run established or proved itself in any other way. Religions have *approved* themselves; they have ministered to sundry vital needs which they found reigning. When they violated other needs too strongly, or when other faiths came which served the same needs better, the first religions were supplanted." [1]

[1] "The Varieties of Religious Experience," p. 331.

Hence the pragmatist is likely to look with a good deal of favor on the "psychology of religion" and to emphasize the human utility of the various religious concepts. Nor does this involve any lack of belief in the religious view of the universe on the part of the pragmatist. He is indeed skeptical of the value of the historical proofs of God, and is the chief antagonist of the idealistic Absolute. Yet, for all that, he is, as a rule, essentially and temperamentally religious, and he has his own arguments for a religious *Weltanschauung*. One of these he finds in the very nature of man and of religion as portrayed by contemporary psychology. Religion goes deeper than do any of its intellectual formulations; it springs not from the abstract reason but from the whole man. It is biological rather than intellectual, and is an almost instinctive reaction of man to his environment. Religious belief of some kind is a normal and almost a necessary human product, and for this reason may be and (in fact) must be trusted. Moreover, our trust in it is justified in the same general way in which scientific hypotheses are justified: it stands the test of usefulness. *It works;* it ministers to human needs; it combines harmoniously, on the whole, with human experience, and it furthers human life and happiness. This, says the pragmatist, is the only kind of verification to be found in science, and though in the case of religion the verification is much less exact and complete, it is essentially of the same nature and is sufficient to justify our trust until positively overthrown. For although the beliefs of religion are as yet only partially verified, that is what one must expect from the enormous magnitude and complexity of religion's problem; and it must be remembered, too, that the relatively simple "laws" and "truths" of science, now universally accepted, were one day in the same position and started out as mere postulates. "Science too takes risks," as Schiller says, "and ventures herself on postulates, hypotheses, and analogies, which seem wild, until they

are tamed to our service and confirmed in
their allegiance. She too must end by saying *Credo ut intelligam*. And she does
this because she must. For, as Professor
Dewey has admirably shown, *all values and
meanings rest upon beliefs*, and, 'we cannot
preserve significance and decline the personal attitude in which it is inscribed and
operative. . . .' We start, then, always from
the postulates of faith, and transmute them,
slowly, into the axioms of reason. The
presuppositions of scientific knowledge and
religious faith are the same." [1]

Pragmatism thus seeks to prove the truth
of religion by its good and satisfactory consequences. Here, however, a distinction
must be made ; namely, between the " good, "
harmonious, and logically confirmatory consequences of religious concepts as such, and
the good and pleasant consequences which
come from believing these concepts. It is
one thing to say a belief is true because the
logical consequences that flow from it fit in

[1] " Studies in Humanism," pp. 361–362.

harmoniously with our otherwise grounded knowledge ; and quite another thing to call it true because it is pleasant to believe. We may conceive, therefore, two perfectly distinct methods of verification through consequences.   The first is exactly that used by science; the second (namely, through consequences which flow not from the idea as such but from our believing it) is very far removed from the scientific method, and is held only by pragmatists — if it be really held even by them.   That it is so held by some at least, would seem to be clear from such expressions as the following: " If theological ideas prove to have a value for concrete life, they will be true, in the sense of being good for so much. "   " So far as the Absolute affords comfort it surely is not sterile, it has that amount of value; it performs a concrete function.   As a good pragmatist I myself ought to call the Absolute true *in so far forth* then; and I unhesitatingly now do so." [1]   It would seem, therefore, that any-

[1] " Pragmatism," p. 73.

thing is true "in so far forth" which it is comfortable to believe. But whether pragmatism really holds this doctrine is doubtful. As Professor Dewey says, "Light would be thrown upon how Mr. James conceives this matter by statements from him on such points as these: If ideas terminate in good consequences, but yet the goodness of the consequences was no part of the intention of the idea, does the goodness have any verifying force? If the goodness of consequences arises from the context of the idea in belief rather than from the idea itself, does it have any verifying force? If an idea leads to consequences which are good in the *one* respect only of fulfilling the intent of the idea (as when one drinks a liquid to test the idea that it is a poison) does the badness of the consequences in every other respect detract from the verifying force of these consequences?"[1]

Certainly if pragmatism means that any-

[1] "What does Pragmatism mean by Practical?" *Jour. of Phil.*, Vol. V, pp. 93–94.

thing may be proved true if the consequences
of believing it are comforting, it is provided
with a very cheap and easy method of demonstration. Pragmatists are always indig-
nant at the common accusation that they
teach us we may believe whatever we like;
but it must be admitted there is considerable excuse, as Professor Dewey has himself
pointed out above, for this interpretation of
their doctrine. However, I shall not press
this point farther nor take seriously the implication that *any* good consequences which
flow from our belief in an hypothesis can be
used to prove its truth. And certainly if
pragmatism does not mean to use this rather
questionable method of verification, but seeks
to demonstrate the truth of religious doctrines
purely from their own proper and necessary
consequences, it is on good logical and scientific ground. How far these consequences
actually do prove the doctrines referred to is,
of course, another question; and it must be
admitted that pragmatism has as yet made
but little serious attempt in concrete detail

to furnish this sort of verification for our religious concepts.

So much for the pragmatist's way of proving the truth of our religious beliefs. But this is only a part of what he has to say in defense of faith. For, he continues, even if the proof of religion be not complete, it is at least as good as that of the opposite view, and therefore, seeing that one must choose between rival hypotheses neither of which can be demonstrated, one has a right to take refuge in the will to believe. For belief, after all, is no mere cold intellectualistic state of mind, but has in it an element of will and of emotion. On vital questions where there is genuine uncertainty one cannot forever keep decision in abeyance. Hence the pragmatist, as a general thing, takes his stand and makes his life venture on the side which promises most if once accepted. Life is better, sweeter, more worthy and worth while with some sort of religious belief than without it; hence, says the pragmatist, since such a belief is at least as well grounded as its rival, let us deliberately adopt it as a working hypothesis until it is discredited.

Thus a road is opened to religious faith even for those who feel (as modern men are coming more and more to feel) that demonstration in religious matters is no longer to be expected. For such men, this is perhaps the only protection against a rather sad skepticism. And it is a protection because it shows that skepticism itself is quite as much a voluntary choice as is the religious attitude. Choose we must, whether we will or no. Says Professor James, in the famous book which is the very Gospel of this Justification of Faith, " We cannot escape the issue by remaining skeptical and waiting for more light, because although we do avoid error in that way, *if religion be untrue*, we lose the good *if it be true*, just as certainly as if we positively choose to disbelieve. . . . Skepticism then is not avoidance of option; it is option of a certain particular kind of risk. *Better risk loss of truth than chance of error* — that is your faith-vetoer's exact position. He is

actively playing his stake as much as the believer is; he is backing the field against the
religious hypothesis, just as the believer is
backing the religious hypothesis against the
field. To preach skepticism to us as a duty
until 'sufficient evidence' for religion be
found, is tantamount, therefore, to telling us,
when in the presence of the religious hypothesis, that to yield to our fear of its being
error is wiser and better than to yield to our
hope that it may be true. . . . And dupery
for dupery, what proof is there that dupery
through hope is so much worse than dupery
through fear? I, for one, can see no proof;
and I simply refuse obedience to the scientist's command to imitate his kind of option,
in a case where my own stake is important
enough to give me the right to choose my
own form of risk. If religion be true and
the evidence for it be still insufficient, I do
not wish by putting your extinguisher upon
my nature (which feels to me as if it had
after all some business in this matter) to for-
feit my sole chance in life of getting upon the

winning side — that chance depending, of course, on my willingness to run the risk of acting as if my passional need of taking the world religiously might be prophetic and right." [1]

This, as I have said, is the position taken by most pragmatists. That it is so is due to the general tendencies of their disposition and temperament, rather than to any logical and necessary connection between it and their epistemology. Nor is it by any means peculiar to them. It was already old long before pragmatism was born, and is to-day enthusiastically supported by many pronounced antagonists of pragmatism. Cicero voiced something very like it when he said he would rather be wrong with Plato than right with Plato's opponents. And every one will remember that Kant came even nearer to the " will to believe " when he destroyed knowledge in order to substitute faith. It was, of course, this general point of view that prompted his advocacy of the primacy

[1] " The Will to Believe," pp. 26–27.

o

of the practical reason and his moral argument for God. This same attempt to found religion on the moral will was carried farther by Fichte and still farther by Ritschl. The merit of Professor James's brilliant book lay not so much in its originality, as in its giving this century-old doctrine a broader philosophical setting and foundation, by showing that not only religious belief but nearly all belief is in part a matter of will, and in presenting the right to believe in a form at once so persuasive and so inspiring. I think I shall be justified in saying that James's " Will to Believe " has been one of the greatest influences for genuine religious faith that have appeared in the last half century.

So much for the religious views actually held by many pragmatists. And now for the less interesting but really more important attempt to work out the logical consequences of pragmatic epistemology as applied to religious problems. Our question therefore is not, What attitude does the pragmatist usually take? but What attitude *ought* he to take if he is going to be faithful to his own presuppositions?

I have said that the view which holds the beliefs of religion to be true because of their value for life, and which maintains that we have a right to believe them even when unverified, is not peculiar to pragmatism, and that it does not follow from the fundamental principles concerning knowledge, truth, and meaning which alone are uniquely pragmatic. But one must go farther than this: and, in fact, the thesis which I shall seek to maintain will be that it is logically inconsistent to proclaim and carry out the more extreme and radical pragmatic principles, and at the same time cling to the religious view of the universe and seek to uphold genuine belief in it.

The extreme pragmatist view, if I understand it aright, maintains that the meaning of any philosophic proposition can always be brought down to some particular consequence in human experience. A true belief

if it has any meaning always " has a bearing
on some human interest." " Theoretical
truth is no relation between our mind and
the archetypal reality. It falls *within* the
mind, being the accord of some of its processes and objects with other processes and
objects." It is " an experienced relation," or
" the effective working of an idea," or the
process of the idea's verification. Hence all
genuine meaning and all truth (and, of
course, all knowledge as well) lie within the
individual's experience, or, at the broadest,
within the experience of the human race.
The beliefs of religion, on the other hand, —
the very beliefs for which we have seen the
pragmatists so valiantly fighting, — are
largely concerned with matters which by
their nature lie beyond the limits of human
experience. Primal among these, for example, is the belief in a God, — not merely
in future experiences of yours and mine
which will be " the same as if " there were a
God, but in the actual present existence of a
divine being who by definition is not within

the experience of any or all of us. Whatever the pragmatists may mean by God, this at least is what the religious man means by the term and what the pragmatist is naturally supposed to mean when arguing for the religious hypothesis. And it must be clear to every one that if all truth and meaning are confined to consequences within our human experience, we are deprived of all right to talk about and believe in a being who by the very conditions of the argument is not included within our experience.

To this the pragmatist will reply that the very peculiarities of the pragmatic epistemology which I have pointed out make it really the only sure salvation from philosophic doubt. All other views of truth and knowledge but his own, the pragmatist will maintain, are by their nature doomed to end in skepticism. For once admit the necessity of transcendence, the existence of a chasm between your idea and its object, and you have made knowledge forever impossible. Knowledge is possible and skepticism vanquished

only for a theory which denies the existence
of any chasm and the necessity of any transcendence.   This is exactly what pragmatism
does.   It points out that the whole of your
genuine meaning can always be summed up
in some possible difference in your own (or
other human) life; that truth is only a concrete process within the mind; and that
knowledge is a succession of the doubt-inquiry-answer type and "lives wholly inside
the tissue of experience." Hence your idea
and its object are not separated by any chasm,
but are both parts of the same chain and
united by intermediaries of the same nature.
Your idea therefore may genuinely know its
object and may be proved true since its truth
consists just in its satisfactory working.   Apply this now to religion, and all becomes clear.
" If theological ideas prove to have a value
for concrete life, they will be true in the
sense of being good for so much." " On prag-
matistic principles if the hypothesis of God
works satisfactorily in the widest sense of
the word, it is true." [1]   Of course, you must

[1] " Pragmatism," pp. 73 and 299.

consider with care the question whether it
does really work satisfactorily; but if it does,
that is all you mean by its being true, and
thus the chasm and the need of transcendence is avoided.

Thus pragmatism attempts to save us from
philosophic doubt by making knowledge,
truth, and meaning have their entire being
within the tissue of human experience.   But
it was not the things within human experience which we were ever tempted to doubt.
It was the things outside human experience, — God, immortality, the moral nature
of the universe, the final victory of the right,
— it was of these we felt doubtful.   And
how does pragmatism help us here?   It does
not pretend to tell us what our future experience will be, much less to declare to us the
things that are outside all possible human
experience.   Its message is really this : You
may believe there is a God because all you
mean by a God is certain "adjustments of
our attitudes of hope and expectation."   A
" vague confidence in the future is the sole

pragmatic meaning at present discernible in the terms design and designer." "Other than this practical significance, the words God, free will, design, have none." [1]

"When I affirm that the metaphysical theory of the Absolute is *false*," says Schiller, "I only mean that it is *useless*, that it simplifies nothing and complicates everything." [2] And the consistent pragmatist, of course, holds the converse of this; namely, that when he affirms that the theory of God is *true* he means only that it is *useful*, that it simplifies things within experience — *not that there really is* a God. This (if I understand him) is the avowed attitude of Professor Dewey, and it certainly is the only logical and consistent attitude of any pragmatist who takes his own doctrines of truth and meaning seriously.

Of course, this view of religion is not what the reading public understands the pragmatist to mean when he so bravely tells us we have a right to believe in God.

[1] "Pragmatism," pp. 115, 121.   [2] "Humanism," p. 59.

There is a general impression abroad that pragmatism has somehow discovered a short cut to God and religion which makes skepticism no longer tenable, and that if one ever became a real philosophical pragmatist, one would understand what it was. And in fact nearly all the pragmatists themselves, except perhaps Professor Dewey and some of his followers, at times feel the need of something more solid and objective than the sort of " God " one comes to by strict pragmatic principles. Thus at the close of his " Varieties of Religious Experience," Professor James points out that one's " subjective way of feeling things " is not all one wants from religious beliefs; one wants to know also about the " objective truth of their content "; and he adds in a note, " The word ' truth ' is here taken to mean something additional to bare value for life." [1] The attempt of Professor James to prove the old-fashioned God by the new-fashioned argument is well criticised by

[1] p. 509.

Professor Dewey in the admirable article
from which I have already quoted. "Consider," he says, "the case of design. Mr.
James begins by accepting a ready-made
notion, to which he then applies the pragmatic criterion. The traditional notion is
that of a 'seeing force that runs things.'
This is rationalistically and retrospectively
empty; its being there makes no difference.
But 'returning with it into experience, we
gain a more confiding outlook on the future.
If not a blind force but a seeing force runs
things, we may reasonably expect better
issues. *This vague confidence in the future
is the sole pragmatic meaning at present discernible in the terms design and designer'*
[quoted from James]. Now," Dewey continues, "is this intended to *replace* the meaning of a 'seeing force which runs things'?
Or is it intended to superadd a pragmatic
value and validation to that concept of a seeing force? Or does it mean that, irrespective of the existence of any such object, *a
belief in it* has that value? Strict prag-

matism would seem to require the first interpretation, but I do not think that is what Mr. James intends."

Professor Dewey then takes up the question of theism and materialism. Strict pragmatism would tell us that the only meaning of theism lies in the differences it makes to us, and would therefore *substitute* these concrete experiential differences for the old view of God as a "superhuman power," and would, as Dewey says, "simply *abolish* the meaning of an antecedent power."[1]

In short, we have in the common, loose, pragmatic treatment of religion another illustration of the tendency to smuggle in " intellectualistic " results to fill out the deficiencies left by pragmatic methods. "When God is presented as the name of an experienced fact, and theistic theories are taken as methods of interpreting that fact for purposes of response, we are on

[1] "What does Pragmatism mean by Practical?" pp. 90 and 91.

good pragmatic ground.   But when it is declared that 'On pragmatist principles if the hypothesis of God works satisfactorily in the widest sense of the word it is true,' the implication to the innocent reader is far otherwise.   We can hardly put the same eloquence into the naked pragmatic assertion, 'If the hypothesis of God works satisfactorily in the widest sense of the word it *does* work satisfactorily in the widest sense of the word.'   God as an addition to an already smoky image of reality at large, God as an æsthetic anticipation of what visual and other experiences we may have face to face when we have passed over the river, God in these simple 'copy' ways of considering our ideas must be omitted.   God must be the name of a fact in our experience, and the determination of His ways must be the determination of our way of working out our wills in the light of that fact." [1]

[1] Max Eastman in "The Pragmatic Meaning of Pragmatism," a paper read before the Psychological Section of the New York Academy of Sciences.

The logical outcome of pragmatism, therefore, when applied to religion is not salvation from philosophic doubt, but a necessary
and ineradicable skepticism.   This, indeed,
might have been foreseen from the outset.
We shall recognise it clearly enough if, with
the light we have now attained, we read over
again some of its fundamental principles.
Take, for example, its chief "postulate," as
presented by Professor Dewey.   " Things —
anything, everything, in the ordinary or
non-technical use of the term thing — are
what they are experienced as.   Hence if
one wishes to describe anything truly, his
task is to tell what it is experienced as
being."   " The real significance of the principle is that of a method of philosophical
analysis.   If you wish to find out what subjective, objective, physical, mental, cosmic,
psychic, cause, substance, purpose, activity,
evil, being, quantity — any philosophical
term in short — means, go to experience and
see what it is experienced as."   And, the
pragmatist would of course continue, God

and the other objects of religion are what
we experience them as, and (for us and our
belief at least) nothing more.   Certain aspects
of our experience is all they can *mean* for us.
And it is the same with their truth.   Since the
truth of an idea means merely the fact that the
idea works, that fact is all you mean when you
say the idea is true.   Nothing more, nothing "transcendent" nor "cosmic" must be
sought from it.   It is a very simple matter,
you see, — like the multiplication table, —
"we simply fill the hole with the dirt we
dug out.   Why are twice two four?   Because, in fact, four is twice two."   It is thus a
very easy thing to prove our belief in God to
be true by the good consequences that flow
from it, because all we mean by God is just
those good consequences.   The real outcome of pragmatism is therefore an assurance that the questions in which ordinary
religious people are interested are essentially
insoluble, — hopelessly insoluble, in fact,
because of the very nature of knowledge and
truth and meaning, — and that we should

therefore go about our business and fulfill as an hireling our day. For, as Professor Dewey says, " The appropriate subject-matter of awareness is not reality at large, a metaphysical heaven to be mimeographed at many removes upon a badly constructed mental carbon paper which yields at best only fragmentary, blurred, and erroneous copies. Its proper and legitimate object is that relationship of organism and environment in which functioning is most amply and effectively attained; or by which, in case of obstruction and consequent needed experimentation, its later eventual free course is most facilitated. As for the other reality, metaphysical reality at large, it may, so far as awareness is concerned, go to its own place." [1]

This consignment of all questions about reality at large which do not directly concern the functioning of the organism to their " own place " (which may be anywhere you

[1] " Does Reality Possess Practical Character? " in the Columbia *Festschrift* for James, pp. 70–71.

like except amongst suitable subjects for
human discussion) is perfectly justified by,
and, in fact, is the only logical conclusion
from the fundamental principles of pragmatism. For if these principles be correct, 'tis
idle for us creatures of a day, who cannot
even *mean* anything beyond our own experience, to spend our time on questions necessarily so remote and inaccessible as are those
which religious people *think* they are discussing and about which they *think* they
care. From them we are separated by a
chasm much more impossible to pass than
that which the rationalists seek to bridge
with their method of transcendence. For if
pragmatism be true, it is not a chasm, but an
infinite stretch of empty space that bounds
each of us — or at least the race — on every
hand, so that if there be another side we at
least can neither know nor even mean it.
On such an epistemology the discussion of
the old problems of religion becomes essentially a silly waste of time and gray matter,
which might better be spent in tilling the

soil and nourishing our psychophysical
organism. " The Infinite, the Eternal, the
All-good — *these* are names empty of all real
meaning, idle fancies for minds that will
dream or idly speculate instead of seeking to
know and to make better the only real world
there is, the world of experience. This
world admits no reference to a superhuman
reality. We are thus left with reality that is
fragmentary only, with experience that is
made up of flying, ever changing moments,
with thought that never wins final truth,
with temporal processes and no eternal
to justify and give them meaning; with
finite progress and no goal finally won;
with a better and no best as the ultimate
standard of value judgments. For the satisfaction of ethical and religious ideals and
aspirations we must look to our possibly
better selves. Our idealized selves are our
gods; and the cry after the Divine, the
Eternal, the Complete in knowledge and
goodness, must be satisfied with that frag-
ment of truth and goodness which is all

P

that our finite lives can possess in their best estate." [1]

Of course, this is not what most pragmatists actually hold. But it is, I maintain, the logical outcome of their fundamental principles — the principles which alone are peculiar to their philosophy. In short, if strictly carried out to its logical conclusions, pragmatism is essentially a philosophy of skepticism. Or better still, perhaps, in Papini's naïve and ingenuous expression, " Pragmatism is really less a philosophy than a method of doing without one."

[1] Professor Russell, "Objective Idealism and Revised Empiricism — Discussion," *Phil. Rev.*, Vol. XV, p. 633.

LECTURE VI

THE "PRACTICAL" POINT OF VIEW

LECTURE VI

THE "PRACTICAL" POINT OF VIEW

"HOWSOEVER these things are in men's depraved judgments and affections, yet truth, which only doth judge itself, teacheth that the inquiry of truth, which is the love-making or wooing of it; the knowledge of truth, which is the presence of it; and the belief of truth, which is the enjoying of it, is the sovereign good of human nature." These words of Francis Bacon contain within them the ultimate justification of all philosophy. Whoever accepts them will hold that philosophical investigation is an end in itself, needing no apology or defense; while to the man who challenges them most philosophy will seem but a sorry waste of energy.

The present controversy over pragmatism may at times appear to the non-technical

reader a battle between ghosts and shad-
ows, a smoky discharge of weightless pro-
jectiles, a ridiculously noisy war of words
in a realm so far removed from the world
of real life as to be quite out of touch with
any genuine human interest. And even
those of us who have somehow got en-
tangled in the struggle feel now and then
(*crede experto*) a disheartening doubt that
perhaps the game is not worth the candle
after all, and that maybe our manuscripts
were better used for building fires and
baking bread. This sense of uncertainty,
however, and of the possible worthlessness
of one's efforts, is not peculiar to those
involved in the pragmatist controversy.
Doubt of the same discouraging sort is
apt to come at times upon every one en-
gaged in theoretical pursuits of any nature
and make him question seriously and sadly
the value of his work. The Spirit that
Denies is not far from any one of us, and
is ever ready with his disconcerting suggestion, " It may be clever, but is it worth

while?" At such moments it is well to turn back to our Francis Bacon and read again the comforting words of the father of English philosophy. They bring back courage to our hearts as the touch of earth renewed the strength of Antæus. The possession of truth *is* "the sovereign good of human nature." We again feel sure that this is so; for "truth, which alone doth judge itself, teacheth" it. To make "an unusually obstinate attempt to think clearly and consistently,"[1] to carry out our thoughts to their logical conclusions, to see what we really mean and must mean by knowledge and truth, these may be peculiarly difficult and dreary tasks, but they are worth our while if the possession of truth is worth our while. The pragmatist controversy is not logomachy nor is it unimportant. If the traditional view of truth and knowledge is meaningless, as the pragmatists contend, then we ought to know it, and not slumber on in dogmatic confidence

---

[1] James's famous definition of metaphysics.

that our old bottles will stand the strain
of the new wine which modern logic and
modern science are pouring into them. If
new bottles are necessary, by all means let
us have them before the old ones perish
and the wine be spilt. And if, on the
other hand, the pragmatist substitutes for
our older concepts are self-contradictory and
land us in absurd and untenable positions,
that too we ought to know. For clear thinking is worth while for its own sake, and
knowledge of the truth "is the sovereign
good of human nature."

Nor is the aim of either the pragmatists
or their opponents merely controversial.
At times it may seem so, but this appearance is merely superficial. To get the
better of the other side is merely an inci-
dental aim, and deep down below this runs
the genuine and serious desire of both
parties to get at the truth for its own sake.
In a very real sense there is no controversy
here but an investigation, there are not
two parties but one, and the aim of all con-

cerned is to give each other mutual aid in the common search. The non-pragmatists genuinely wish to see pragmatism completely developed and clearly expressed, and the pragmatists welcome all criticism, adverse or favorable, knowing that this will only aid them in thinking out their own thoughts logically and to the end. We are really partners rather than opponents, each seeking the same thing, each making common cause with the rest, and each wishing the other Godspeed.

In man's long search after truth — "the lovemaking and wooing of it," as Bacon would say — it is possible to make out two chief tendencies or types of attitude. One class of mind has been so carried away with the joy of mental achievement, so enchanted by the glory of truth, that in seeking and proclaiming it as the supreme end of life it has quite overlooked the fact that truth is not only an end but a means as well; that it not only is a good, but also is good for something. The other type of truth-seeker, noting the error of overemphasis on truth merely as an end, has sought to counterbalance this mistake by laying its emphasis upon the practical value of truth and its possession; pointing out that truth and knowledge are means to all sorts of other good things, that they are tools and implements which should be used as well as enjoyed, and that in our enthusiasm over the possession of these things, the humbler practical values of life must not be slighted.

It is to this latter tendency that pragmatism belongs and it is to this broad, living, human point of view that it owes its rather striking popularity and the rapid progress that it has made among non-technical readers. For certainly it is not the special technical doctrines of pragmatism that have aroused so much real interest among the reading public. There is no great spontaneous curiosity in the community at large concerning the interpretation of the terms "meaning," "truth," and "knowledge." It

is rather the pragmatist's large, big-hearted,
practical way of looking at things that has
attracted the general attention to what he
has to say. The reading public is seldom
interested in the technical and exact side of
any science or discipline. It naturally and
quite properly hates exactness. It likes
X-rays and electrons and geological periods
and light years and the survival of the fittest; but when it comes to technical methods and exact descriptions and definitions,
it "wants to be excused." And, therefore,
it loves pragmatism not as a technical philosophical doctrine, but as an interesting,
belligerent, "practical" point of view.

As such, however, pragmatism is, as I
have said, only a part of a larger tendency,
— a tendency which, though one of the
most important characteristics of contemporary thought, is rather difficult to name or
define. It might be called the *empirical* or
the *biological* or the *historical* or, perhaps,
simply the *practical* point of view. It has
permeated so much of our thinking and has

taken on so many shades and aspects that it has no longer very much unity except as a general "psychological atmosphere," and also, perhaps, as a universal protest against the point of view which it opposes and has in part replaced. To make more plain what I have in mind, it will be necessary to say a few words about this prior point of view, which may be called (for want of a better name) that of excessive intellectualism.

By this I mean, of course, the tendency already pointed out, which considers truth only as an end and never as a means, and so in part divorces truth and knowledge from the world of active and practical life. This way of conceiving things probably antedates history. It had no father, and it seems to have dominated in large part the thought of many of the ancient philosophers. The most famous of its early representatives was, of course, Plato.[1] For his severance of the

---

[1] It should also be pointed out, however, that there is a decidedly pragmatic tendency in Plato, inherited from his spiritual father, Socrates, and seen especially in his doctrine of the Idea of the Good.

world of "illusion" from the "real" world of
Ideas, however great its value in some respects, was certainly the first long step
toward the separation of "true knowledge"
from the practical world of action and concrete experience.   And, immeasurable as is
Plato's gift to philosophy, it cannot be denied
that his sharp separation of our meanings
from our individual, living experience, in
which alone they are genuinely real, was
fatal for both.   The inaccessible and changeless world of abstract concepts, which Plato
is at least supposed to have believed in, was
erected for the purpose of explaining the
changing world which we actually experience, and the chasm which was made between them defeated the very purpose for
which the two had been distinguished.   The
purely and abstractly logical and intellectualistic, purified from all human taint, was
so completely divorced from the emotional
and volitional, from the struggle and endeavor of concrete, pulsing actuality, that
it became next to useless as a means of

rationalizing the world of our actual human experience. And while philosophy was constructing this purely "ideal" realm, an abstract psychology was dividing man's mind into three sharply sundered faculties, and not only made reason supreme (as indeed it should), but abstractly "pure" and independent.

How far the above is a statement of Plato's philosophy and how far a caricature of it, is a question which for our present purposes is irrelevant; for this at least is the interpretation of his meaning which has had most influence in the history of human thought. And it resulted in an exaltation of the abstract intellect and a contempt for the "passions" and feelings, the impulses and will attitudes of man, which dominated thought for two thousand years. Man was regarded and defined as a "thinking animal." That he was an animal was most unfortunate; for thought, "pure" thought, was his "essence." The animal nature of man was hardly worthy of investigation, the proper study of mankind being the abstract "Universals" of mediæval "Realism."

Other influences besides that of Plato were brought to bear in this direction, — in fact, almost every philosopher for more than a thousand years contributed his share. Aristotle's was certainly too catholic a nature, too empirical a mind, to be a slave to any such excessive intellectualism; yet his thought was so interpreted and his work so used that for centuries his influence also tended to bind philosophy and science in intellectualistic fetters. This was largely due, of course, to his placing the "theoretical reason" far above the "practical reason." The syllogism, moreover, which he had contrived as a practical tool for man's use was made a fetish, and elaborated for its own sake. And the questions upon which it was used and to which most scholastic thinkers devoted their lives were sadly remote from human experience. Doubtless the abstractions and absurdities of mediæval thinkers have been greatly and unfairly exaggerated; yet, when all is said, it must be admitted that their views of man's nature and of man's problems were often false in the extreme, and their quibbles and logomachy, their absurd interest in purely verbal questions, their expenditure of years upon mere fantastic puzzles, meant a pitiful and irreparable waste of really great intellectual power.

The point of view of excessive intellectualism did not die with the mediæval schoolmen. It has its representatives to-day, and it is against this tendency to worship the purely abstract intellect and its artificial problems that the modern spirit in general, and pragmatism in particular, protest. The newer point of view made its appearance in philosophy long, long ago; but from the growth of the natural sciences in the last century, the development of the historical sense, and especially the spread of biological ideas, it has taken new strength and even a new form. The attitude of the age is expressed by the motto, "Knowledge is *power*." The suitable subjects for human investigation are seen to be those which belong to this very world in which we live, and to our actual experience, — the problems whose answers will make a real difference to us. Already two hundred years ago it was perceived that "the proper study of mankind is man"; and now that man has come to be studied seriously, empirically, scientifically, it is seen that he is a very different sort of creature from that which scholasticism painted him. A "thinking animal," if you like, he is indeed; but the modern conception puts the emphasis on the "animal" rather than on the "thinking." For, as it views him, man is not an animal in order that he may think; he thinks in order that he may be a better animal. Life is no longer conceived as existing for the sake of knowledge; knowledge exists for the sake of life. Thought is not the "essence" of man, nor is it for its own sake. It is merely one of man's tools by which he may

Q

the better react upon his environment, and
therefore stands upon the same plane as his
eyes and his stomach. It was developed by
the struggle for existence according to the
law of the survival of the fittest, for the definite purpose of guiding the organism and
so of helping to preserve the individual and
to perpetuate the race. And contemporary
physiological psychology, adopting the biological point of view, has carried it out in
detail, showing the exact place of thought
in the economy of nature, — its position in
the reflex arc pointing to its sole function;
namely, the guidance of the individual's
action upon the environment. Consciousness is really only a stop-gap for mechanical
action. In the words of an eminent German
psychologist,[1] it is the "defect of habit."
And our own foremost physiological psychologist writes as follows: —

 "The structural unity of the nervous
system is a triad, neither of whose elements
has any independent existence. The sen-

[1] Max Dessoir in "Das Doppel-ich."

sory impression exists only for the sake of awakening the central process of reflection, and the central process of reflection exists only for the sake of calling forth the final act. All action is thus *re*-action upon the outer world; and the middle stage of consideration or contemplation or thinking is only a place of transit, the bottom of a loop, both of whose ends have their point of application in the outer world. If it should ever have no roots in the outer world, if it should ever happen that it led to no active measures, it would fail of its essential function, and would have to be considered either pathological or abortive. The current of life which runs in at our eyes or ears is meant to run out at our hands, feet, or lips. The only use of the thoughts it occasions while inside is to determine its direction to whichever of these organs shall, on the whole, under the circumstances actually present, act in the way most propitious to our welfare." [1]

[1] James, "Reflex Action and Theism," in "The Will to Believe," pp. 113, 114.

The difference between what may be called the intellectualistic and the practical views of thought and knowledge is admirably stated in another passage by the same brilliant writer. To the question, he says, why we must intellectualize, interpret, and understand our originally pure or raw experience, rationalism and pragmatism give different answers. "The rationalistic answer is that the theoretic life is absolute and its interests imperative, and that to understand is simply the duty of man, and that he who questions this need not be argued with, for by the fact of arguing he gives away his case. The pragmatic answer is that the environment kills as well as sustains us, and that the tendency of raw experience to extinguish the experient himself is lessened just in the degree in which the elements in it that have a practical bearing upon life are analyzed out of the continuum and verbally fixed and coupled together, so that we may know what is in the wind for us and get ready to react in time. Had pure experience, the pragmatist says, been always perfectly healthy, there would never have been the necessity of isolating or verbalizing any of its terms. We should just have experienced inarticulately and unintellectually enjoyed. This leaning on 'reaction' in the pragmatist account implies that whenever we intellectualize a relatively pure experience, we ought to do so for the sake of redescending to the purer or more concrete level again; and that if an intellect stays aloft among its abstract terms and generalized relations, and does not reinsert itself with its conclusions into some particular point of the immediate stream of life, it fails to finish out its function and leaves its normal race unrun.

"Most rationalists nowadays will agree that pragmatism gives a true enough account of the way in which our intellect arose at first, but they will deny these later implications. The case, they will say, resembles that of sexual love. Originating in the animal need of getting another genera-

tion born, this passion has developed secondarily such imperious spiritual needs that if
you ask why another generation ought to
be born at all, the answer is : 'Chiefly that
love may go on.'   Just so with our intellect:
it originated as a practical means of serving
life; but it has developed incidentally the
function of understanding absolute truth;
and life itself now seems to be given chiefly
as a means by which that function may be
prosecuted."[1]   All of which the upholders
of the practical or biological point of view
of course deny.

The advantages of this viewpoint are, of
course, too obvious to need enumeration.
It brings down knowledge from the skies
and makes it concrete, useful, and living.
It directs investigation into paths which
lead us to genuine and valuable results.
And it brings about a simplification and
systematization of our knowledge which, to
the scientist, is hard to overvalue.   The

[1] "The Thing and its Relations," *Jour. of Phil.*, Vol. II,
pp. 30-31.

various facts of psychology now get a definite setting and fit in with the biological facts, with a place for everything and everything in its place, like beads on a string. The one great biological purpose — the forwarding of the life of the individual and of the race — is seen to dominate and to determine each detail, and thus makes the whole circle of the life sciences beautifully systematic and complete.

Nor is it the life sciences alone that have thus been systematized and illumined by the newer point of view. The biologists have found it possible to apply their formula to ethics as well; and by the aid of it have sought to throw new light on the meaning of duty and the moral imperative. Thus from them we learn that man's chief end is to put himself in line with the progress of evolution and to make the purpose and aim of evolution his own. This aim and purpose is, we are told, the preservation of the individual and the reproduction and "development" of the race. This is shown by such facts as the following : that the organism is brought to full perfection at the age of reproduction, that after that age is passed degeneration begins to set in, — the teeth decay and fall out, the eye grows less keen, the bodily force is abated, etc., etc. Individual preservation and race reproduction being thus the purpose of the evolutionary process, a "scientific" psychology must interpret all of man's functions in this light. His emotions are for the sake of stimulating him to action, his thought is for the guidance of that action, the action always aiming directly or indirectly at self-preservation or race reproduction. Nothing else is for its own sake ; or, at any rate, if there seem to be other ultimate aims than action, they are either pathological or abortive. Hence knowledge is purely "practical" and for the sake of action, and the end of righteousness and ground of morality is the preservation of the race.

Nor have the physiological psychologists

been behindhand in assisting the biologists
to reformulate our ethical concepts. From
one of the most enthusiastic of their number, for example, I quote the following :—

"Although to-day the old-fashioned dual-
ism of sense and reason has been set aside
in the higher scientific circles, and although
psycho-physiological science is now in a condition to provide the necessary data for a
detailed psycho-physiology of the Moral Imperative," ethics "still continues to waste
its efforts in the quest for the criterion of
conduct." To seek for a moral criterion is
vain, nor is the real truth about the problems of right and wrong to be discovered by
the antiquated and intellectualistic methods of the ethical philosophers. It is to
be gained only by a study of the reflex-arc.
Genuinely to understand the moral imperative, it must be got at from the psycho-
physiological point of view. Such a truly
scientific study shows that "the Moral Imperative is the psychic correlate of a reflective, cerebro-spinal, ideo-motor process, the

efferent end of which is organized into motor tracts coördinated for a specific action." [1]

After what I have said of the over-emphasis in years past upon the abstract intellect and of the great value of the more modern practical point of view, I hope I shall not be accused of doing the latter injustice if I say that in some ways the reaction seems to have gone too far. The last quotation will perhaps illustrate my meaning. The biological tendency of contemporary thought has contributed a great deal of value to our science and philosophy, but like many another excellent tendency it has, in my opinion, been somewhat over-emphasized. It has pressed its splendidly useful and illuminating formulæ too far, it has attempted to simplify too much, and in doing so it has become somewhat narrow, somewhat blind, and somewhat unempirical. Its formulæ are able to explain a great deal

[1] Professor Leuba in "The Psycho-physiology of the Moral Imperative," *Am. Jour. of Psy.*, Vol. VIII, pp. 529–530.

of our reality; but, in our enthusiastic application of them, many things which they do not fit have been either bent out of shape or completely disregarded and left out of account. In fact the whole point and purpose of this lecture is to protest against this excessive practical or biological point of view, and to urge a partial return to something like the old-fashioned intellectualism. I am very far from denying either the excesses to which intellectualism has been carried, or the great value of the newer tendency. The reaction was needed, and it has been wonderfully productive and fruitful. But, to my thinking, the pendulum has now swung too far in the anti-intellectualistic direction.

Especially is this the case with the biological view of morality and knowledge. As to the former I need only point out that it is a very loose kind of reasoning which would hold it possible to determine anything about the highest good and the moral imperative from either the course of evolution or the nature of the reflex-arc. It may be indeed that the "progress" of evolution tends toward the highest good, but if we know this to be so it is because we know independently of the facts of evolution what we *mean* by the highest good. The moral imperative may indeed be "the psychic correlate of a reflective, cerebro-spinal, ideo-motor process," but it is not the moral imperative *because* of its correlation to this fearful and wonderful function. The question how duty is possible, the question what obligation *means*, are hardly answerable by pointing to the reflex-arc. The truth is, in our reaction against scholastic "logic-chopping," description is being substituted for definition, psychology for logic, the *ought* is neglected for the *is*, and questions of meaning are set aside or "answered" by theories of origin. Above all (in "the higher scientific circles" especially), the mighty shibboleth "Evolution" and the facts of physiological psychology are coming to be regarded as having the answer to nearly all real questions. "Development" is the catchword of the times — without too much curiosity as to what we are developing toward, or why we should do it.

Nor should the " practical " view of knowledge go altogether unchallenged. No one, indeed, would any longer deny the practical value of knowledge and thought in guiding the reaction of the individual upon his environment. But when it is maintained that this is the only value to be found in knowledge and reason, that all human values are ultimately matters of action, and that the possession of truth is always a means and never an end in itself, then, as it seems to me, it is time to call a halt and to reassert the old and trite thesis that to know the truth is worth while for its own sake. The whole splendid tradition of humanity's scholars and thinkers from the Greeks to the present day is evidence of this. The existence of pragmatism itself proves it. The noble army of "those who know," from

their master down, rises up to testify to the
fact that knowledge itself, and even apart
from its practical results, is one of the
things most exceedingly worth while. And
not only " worth while " is it; it is as genuinely *human*, as genuinely natural and
normal as is digestion or movement or
reproduction. In the words of "that im-
mortal sentence " of Aristotle's — "*All men
by nature desire knowledge*." [1] Nor can I
here refrain from quoting a little more at
length from "the master of those who know."

" If men philosophized in order to escape
ignorance it is evident that they pursued
wisdom just for the sake of knowing, not
for the sake of any advantage it might
bring. This is shown too by the course
of events. For it is only after practically
all things that are necessary for the comfort
and convenience of life had been provided
that this kind of knowledge began to be
sought. Clearly, then, we pursue this knowledge for the sake of no extraneous use to

[1] "Metaphysics," I, 1.

which it may be put; but, just as we call a man free who serves his own and not another's will, so also this science is the only one of all the sciences that is liberal, for it is the only one that exists for its own sake. . . . More necessary, indeed, every other science may be than this; more excellent there is none."[1]

I have ventured to dwell thus at length on the value of knowledge for its own sake to the human mind because the tendencies of contemporary thought (of which pragmatism is one of the most conspicuous representatives) seem to call for a protest from some one. This is perhaps the first time since the days of Plato when such a protest has been needed. That the possession of reason and of truth was in itself one of the many genuine values of human life, irrespective of what you could do with them, was to our fathers simply a truism. But we, in our enthusiastic assertions that reason is for the sake of life, are almost forgetting

[1] *Ibid.*, I, 2 (Bakewell's Translation).

that reason is a part and a product of life,
— in fact its finest product and " the sovereign good of human nature "—and that
in a very true sense, therefore, life may
also be for the sake of reason.

And I speak of this not only because
the protest seems to me timely and need-
ful, but also because in the modern de-
thronement of reason, the new disregard
of certain old distinctions, and the partial
substitution of psychology for logic, there
is apt to be involved a loss of respect for
careful thought and a decreased endeavor
after logical consistency. In our revolt
against " rationalistic abstractions " and
" pure reason " we are in danger of forgetting that the Principles of Contradiction
and Identity still hold whether we recognize them or not, and that the canons of
Aristotle's Logic cannot be disobeyed with
impunity. We decry the logomachy, the
hair-splitting distinctions, and the "logic-
chopping" of the scholastics; yet it may
well be that in throwing these aside we

are surrendering some of the clear thinking that went with them.

Unless I have quite failed of my purpose
in the preceding lectures, I need bring
forth no further evidence of the dangers
just referred to than pragmatism itself.
Pragmatism is one of the signs of the
times and is perhaps the most typical representative of the tendencies of which I have
been speaking. A brief repetition and sum-
mary of its principal positions will therefore
not be out of place in concluding this, our
final lecture.

Pragmatism has too great contempt for
" logic-chopping " and " hair-splitting distinctions " to be willing to define for us
exactly its view of the nature of meaning.
The meaning of any concept, it assures us,
is limited to the future practical consequences which come from it; — but, as it
turns out, these "*practical* consequences "
mean theoretical ones also; and it is not at
all certain that the "future consequences "
need be future after all. Pragmatism is in-

R

deed fully persuaded that nothing can have
meaning which has not consequences in
some one's experience; but whether this
"some one" refers merely to "ourselves"
or may include sentient beings of the remote past and the distant future, God, and
even purely imaginary beings, we cannot
yet be perfectly sure. The new doctrine of
meaning, on which pragmatism is founded,
therefore amounts to this: that meaning is
somehow or other related to experience,
and probably limited to human experience.
Further than this the pragmatist is prevented from refining, — for fear, apparently,
of chopping logic.

In his treatment of truth the pragmatist
again on principle refuses (or is unable) to
recognize a somewhat subtle but very real
and important distinction; namely, that
between the *meaning* of a thing and the
proof of it, the distinction between the
nature of a relation and *our knowledge* of
it. The assertion that an idea might be
true when not known to be true seems to

him meaningless; nor is he willing to admit any distinction between the truth of an idea and the concrete verification of its truth. When you prove the truth of a thing, the proof and the thing proved are one. In like manner, once you admit that a true idea usually "works," so that you can test its truth by its working, pragmatism immediately concludes that its truth *consists in* its working, that its working is all you mean by its truth. In other words, since *trueness* and *working* usually go together, the two are identified, and we are told that we have here not two concepts but one, and that when we *say* trueness we *mean* working. And the question is not even asked whether the idea is true because it works or works because it is true — the one conception being simply substituted for the other.[1] All of which, in good, old-fashioned, much-derided scholastic language, is a complete confusion

[1] Here I should make exception of Professor James, who, in one passage, says plainly (as has been pointed out) that the idea works because it is true.

hold diametrically opposite views on the same subject and both be said to *know*, provided we are both satisfied and remain satisfied with our respective opinions. Each man thus becomes for himself the measure of all things, and each man has knowledge provided his experience continues to feel satisfactory. And yet the pragmatist is certain that on this question *he* is in possession of knowledge and *you* are not, no matter how you feel about it.

These principles concerning meaning, truth, and knowledge are, as I have said, the presuppositions and foundations of pragmatism. But before bringing these lectures to a close one word more should perhaps be added concerning the general pragmatic view of metaphysics and religion. Before doing this, however, I must make a distinction between the pragmatists; for in their metaphysical and religious attitudes they are far from being of one mind.

Professor James has divided all thinkers into two types, the "tough-minded" and the "tender-minded." The former tend to take the naturalistic, scientific, strictly logical view of the world, uninfluenced by human aspirations and desires. The latter look at things in more idealistic fashion; with them religion and beauty and optimism have more influence than the bare facts of science or the cold results of reasoning. James has also pointed out that pragmatism is a compromise between the two types, sharing in the characteristics of each. This description seems to me most apt, in respect both to the two types in general and to the position of pragmatism in particular. To carry it still further into detail, one might say more specifically that the pragmatist is tough-minded intellectually and tender-minded emotionally; or, better still, perhaps, that he is *tough-minded* and *tender-hearted*. It might, however, be more exact to say that there is really no such being as "the pragmatist," but that there are many pragmatists and that they are divisible roughly into two schools, — the tough-minded and the tender-minded respectively.

rule, afterthoughts which we construct to excuse or buoy up beliefs that originate and subsist quite independently of reasoning. Only, in the case of pragmatism the philosophical presuppositions do not even excuse the belief. The tender-minded pragmatist accepts " God " and the conclusions of a religious metaphysics in much the same way as does the old-fashioned thinker, quite oblivious of the fact that if knowledge be merely experienced transition and truth be merely satisfactory consequences and transcendence be nothing but nonsense, it becomes quite absurd to take the old religious beliefs seriously.

This fact is seen with perfect distinctness by the tough-minded pragmatist. He was, in truth, the first to point it out, nor has he been the last in drawing attention to the inconsistencies of his tender-minded brother. Thus, as we saw in the last lecture, Professor Dewey, with his tough-minded disregard for our prejudices, shows that if we cling to our pragmatist presup-

positions we can no longer mean by "God"
a "seeing force that runs things," but only
a vague expectation of better issues in our
own experience. Both he and James, in
fact, unite in saying: "This vague confidence in the future is the sole pragmatic
meaning at present discernible in the terms
design and designer." For the old notion
of "God" as an antecedent Power who
was and is and is to come, the consistent
pragmatist will carefully "substitute" the
concrete differences which under certain
conditions we shall experience, and he will
"simply abolish the meaning of an antecedent power."

With the same unemotional logic, the
tough-minded pragmatist points out that
the biological view of thought and knowledge leads one inevitably to the same
conclusion and shuts out the hypothetical
objects of metaphysics and theology from
the proper field of human thought. The
mind exists for the purpose of guiding the
reaction of the psycho-physical organism

upon its surroundings, and "its proper and legitimate object is that relationship of organism and environment in which functioning is most amply and effectively attained." The only realities that have or can have any genuine meaning for us are of the "practical" sort. All other "reality" — "metaphysical reality at large" — may, therefore, go to its own place.

By thus deducing the logical consequences of his doctrine the tough-minded pragmatist has put us decidedly in his debt; for now we can see clearly that the pragmatist controversy is not a mere academic discussion, but has truly pragmatic importance. For it opens up the whole question of the nature of man and his position in Reality. Is man indeed what the biological pragmatist considers him — a creature of the environment, a successful animal, whose one aim is practical reaction upon his surroundings? Or is he a twofold being? Is he what the pragmatist describes and, in addition to that, also what

Plato thought him — a citizen of the realm of eternal reason, the *outgrown* ape, who *means* more than he *is*, whose reach should and does exceed his grasp, who " partly is and wholly hopes to be " ?

If the pragmatist is right, if it be true that man cannot mean more than he experiences, that his reach cannot exceed his grasp, if " God " and the " moral nature of the Universe " in the old sense are really meaningless terms, and if all this follows inevitably from the analysis of our meanings and our knowledge, then let us by all means know it, and give in our adherence to the pragmatic and biological view. But let us not accept this analysis too lightly nor without long weighing of its worth, forgetful of the consequences which such acceptance must logically carry in its train. The concepts we have been considering in these lectures may have seemed abstract and lifeless, but the deepest questions of our destiny ultimately hang upon them. And the attitude which we shall adopt toward the pragmatist principles will, if we be consistent, determine our whole philosophy, our whole outlook upon life and upon the world. If this fact be clearly grasped I am sure no further excuse need be pleaded for the difficult and, I fear, dreary discussions that I have led you through during the course of these lectures.

INDEX